This book is dedicated to the memory of workmen, relations and friends of Prestwick Colliery.

To Karen, Fiona and Nicola, my daughters, without whose help this book could never have been written.

To Ann, my wife, whose love, charm and humour kept me on the straight and narrow.

And to all others who contributed in any way.

Beneath this Green and Pleasant Land

A Miner's Life

John Graham

Tyne Bridge Publishing

All the illustrations were drawn by Judy Collins.

All views expressed in this book are solely those of the author and in no way reflect the views of the Council of the City of Newcastle upon Tyne.

©John Graham, 2009

Published by
City of Newcastle upon Tyne
Newcastle Libraries & Information Service
Tyne Bridge Publishing, 2009

www.tynebridgepublishing.co.uk

www.newcastle.gov.uk/libraries

For a free catalogue of Tyne Bridge Publishing books contact:
Tyne Bridge Publishing
Newcastle Libraries
PO Box 88
Newcastle upon Tyne
NE99 1DX
email: tynebridge@newcastle.gov.uk
tel: 0191 2774174

ISBN: 978 1 85795 143 1

Printed by Athenaeum Press, Gateshead

Contents

Preface: A miner's son

I am a miner's son, born in a pit row cottage in the shadow of the winding wheels of an East Northumberland colliery. As a sea cadet I dreamed of a career in the navy, but when my father died from cancer when I was just ten years old, I wasn't left with much in the way of career choice. To help support my beloved mother, I would have to follow the family tradition and work down the pit.

At 15 I left the village school and persuaded the manager at the local Prestwick Colliery to give me a start. One of my finest moments was handing over my first pay packet to my proud mum to supplement her meagre ten shillings widow's pension.

I worked all my life in coal mining until I took early retirement in 1987. But I have never forgotten my 34 years in mining. I was often asked if I suffered from claustrophobia and I never did, but I experienced many different kinds of fear. I have been trapped on a coalface, pinned down and unable to move in a roof fall. I have been cut off at the bottom of the shaft, unable to get to the surface due to a power failure. I have seen the deadly methane gas deliberately ignited underground. I have lived with the constant fear of redundancy as pits were closed. I have witnessed terrible accidents underground and even had a man die in my arms. I have worked in conditions that were so treacherous that I have sweated with fear. And on several occasions I could have been killed or maimed but Lady Luck or the Good Lord smiled on me.

John Graham

1 A new lad at the pit

I was born on Wednesday 13th July 1938 in the village of Prestwick, Northumberland, seven miles north-west of Newcastle. Prestwick was, and still is, a very small community. It consisted of a coal mine, two farms, a small shop and a railway line. Two miles north is Ponteland, where I went to school.

I cannot remember much about the house I was born in as I was only two years old when we moved from the village to Prestwick Terrace, a row of 12 houses adjacent to the railway line and colliery. We moved because the new house had a third bedroom and a 'proper' bath in the scullery, or back-kitchen. There were eight of us in the family, Mam, Dad, two sisters, three brothers and myself, all living at home. I was the second youngest. Ken was the newborn baby.

For Dad to secure the house my two eldest brothers Cyril (18) and Reg (16), who worked on the farm, had to go to work in the colliery. The house did not belong to the colliery, it belonged to the 'Ponteland Trust', but as the colliery manager was a trustee it was through his influence that we obtained the house. Dad was much respected by the colliery manager because of his experience both during and between the wars.

At 16, Dad ran away from home to fight for his King and country in World War I. He was only able to join the Army (the Durham Light Infantry) by giving a false age. While fighting in France he was gassed. Later he was severely wounded in the leg by shrapnel. The bleeding was so bad that at the command to retreat he was going to be left to die – there was no Red Cross, first aid or transport to ferry him to safety.

However, one of his friends refused to leave him and, with help, strapped him onto a gun carriage as they made their way back to the trenches. He received first aid and was later shipped back to England where he recovered in a London hospital.

Eventually he became secretary of the local miners' union. In 1926 he led the local miners in the bitter struggle during the General Strike. He did not work for the whole of the 26 weeks. Two of his brothers black-legged and returned to work after 12 weeks, as did most of his friends.

After the strike ended the miners returned to work, under worse conditions than they had had before. They also received less pay.

Dad, as a strike leader, was not reinstated and could not get a job in any of the surrounding coal mines. This was his punishment. He eventually got a job but only because no one else was prepared to work in such atrocious conditions. He was working in a thin seam of coal, lying on his side throughout the shift, with water constantly streaming down and soaking him. He also had to cycle 12 miles a day to get there and back.

Cycling home from work one night, still drenched to the skin, he was overtaken by a car driven by the manager of his former colliery. Noticing that Dad's work clothes were in such a terrible state the manager pulled over and asked what on earth he had been doing, to which Dad replied: 'Working for a decent living.' Dad went on to tell him how and why he was working like this. Aghast the manager replied: 'If you fancy a job working for me come and see me next Monday.' 'I'm seeing you now,' said Dad. 'OK' replied the manager, 'start at Prestwick at 7am on Monday.'

Prestwick was one of the two collieries he managed, the other was East Walbottle. Dad had previously been the Union Representative at East Walbottle. Both collieries not only had the same manager but also the same union. The men now running the union were all blacklegs during the strike, and now Dad was being asked to serve on a union committee, run by blacklegs! He rejoined the union but refused to serve under them. Eventually, after much persuasion, he accepted the post of Honorary Benevolent Secretary and fought for the men who were owed

Mam and dad. Dad's photograph shows him aged 49. Mam is 21.

compensation due to illness or injury.

Vesting Day, 1947, when all Britain's collieries were nationalised, was one of the proudest days in Dad's life. I was only nine years old at the time but can vividly remember standing alongside him on the railway siding, holding his hand as the National Coal Board flag was raised above the 'heapstead' pulley wheels.

Between the wars Dad nearly died of pneumonia. He eventually died from cancer in 1948. I was ten years old. A few weeks before he died, I was playing out in the back lane when my sister Ethel came looking for me. 'Mam wants you,' she said. I went running into the house to find Mam crying. 'Dad wants to talk to you,' she sobbed. 'Why's Mam crying Dad?' I asked. 'I'm going away for a long time son and I want you to promise me you'll look after her.' 'Where you going Dad?' The more questions I asked the harder Mam cried. Dad was holding my right hand clasped in both of his. He was trying to tell me he was dying. Later, Mam told us that on his death bed he hummed the tune of 'Now is the hour for me to say goodbye,' and then peacefully drifted away. It still brings a lump to my throat every time I hear that song.

The only money coming into the house after Dad died was Mam's widow's pension, ten shillings a week. In order to make ends meet, she went out charring. To help her out I got a job as a butcher's boy delivering meat on a Saturday morning. I did this from the age of ten until I left school at 15. I was paid the princely sum of six shillings. Mr Bewick wanted me to become his full-time assistant but I had other ideas. However, I shall always remember him with deep affection and gratitude for the financial help he gave to our family in times of need.

After Dad died our free coal allowance ceased. So, to provide heat for cooking and washing, Mam, my younger brother Ken and I went to the local stone 'tip' to pick out the coals that had been discarded with the stones. On reflection, Mam must have been a very strong woman. I cannot imagine women of today picking coals by hand, putting them into a sack and carrying them almost 200 yards to our house, especially not at 55 years of age. Mam was very much respected in our village. One of my most affectionate memories of her is of her very high-pitched infectious laugh. Sometimes she would laugh so long and loud that it brought tears to her eyes.

I left school in July 1953 with no academic qualifications. The only course open to me was to go to work in the mines, as all the men in my family had done before me. I was interested in joining the Royal Navy, but with no father to provide for the family it was my duty to stay at home and help Mam. I left school on the Friday and started work on the following Monday, after an interview with the colliery manager on the Saturday morning.

My eldest brother, Cyril, took me along to the manager's office. 'This is John,' said our Cyril. The manager peered at me over the top of his half-moon spectacles. 'And what do you want lad?' he said. 'I want to be an electrician,' I replied. 'An electrician' he scowled, 'I don't need electricians. It's a putter I'm after.' (A putter was someone who pushed coal tubs to and from the coalface to a point known locally as the 'flat', where they would then be hauled up to the surface using ropes). 'Anyway, if I train you to become an electrician you'll have to go to the area pool of electricians and you might not come back to this colliery. You wouldn't like that would you?' I nodded in agreement. 'Start on Monday morning in the screening sheds, seven o'clock sharp. If you turn out to be half as good a worker as your Dad was you'll do.'

The screening sheds were on the surface. They were where the coals were graded. The job of a screener was to pick out the stones that were mixed in with the coal. The reason why I had to start work on the screens was that I was too young to work underground. For this you had to be 16. I was still only 15.

I left the manager's office, with Cyril still talking to the manager, and ran all the way home to tell Mam that I'd got the job. I hardly slept at all over the weekend, I was so excited. I woke up on Monday morning at six o'clock to find that Mam had got me a blue boiler suit, a pair of navy blue knee-length socks, a new pair of hobnailed boots, a pair of dark blue football shorts and a shirt. The clothes were hung over the large oven door, airing. I washed my face and hands (always in cold water), had my breakfast (two bacon sandwiches and a pot of tea), then off I went to my first day's work, carrying with me my new enamelled can of tea and eight sandwiches for my bait.

To get to work all I had to do was to walk up the garden path, cross over the railway line and I was in the pit yard. It took less than a minute. I climbed the very steep steel stairway to the top of the shaft. Looking back towards the house I could see Mam standing at the back door drying her eyes on her pinny and waving. I suddenly felt a warm glow inside me. Now I was the real man of the house.

There were two of us starting work that day, myself and Bill T. We were mates and had also started school on the same day. We had to report to the check weighman and the foreman. His main job was to weigh the tubs of coal as they arrived at the surface and record the weights. This was because the men were paid by the amount of coal they had produced. There were two jobs available that morning, one on the screens and one on the heapstead cleaning out the coal tubs. I was sent to the screens and Bill got the job of cleaning out the wooden coal tubs. I was disappointed at getting the screen job because, as a youngster growing up in the pit yard, I knew what it entailed.

The screens consisted of an endless overhead conveyor belt built on stilts. It carried the coals from the heapstead (the top of the shaft) to the screening plant, a building also on stilts to allow the railway wagons underneath. Inside the plant, the conveyors loaded the coals onto a steel plate which had holes of two different dimensions in it. This separated the coal into two different sizes and placed them on a level lower than the overhead conveyor. My job was to sit on a piece of wood between the conveyors, pick off the stones as they passed and throw them into a hopper. It was a noisy, dusty and extremely boring job, normally done by much older men who, because of ill-health or injury, were no longer able to work underground. It was classed by management as light-work.

Not all of the men who worked in the screening sheds had previously worked underground. One real old character was Geordie. He used to operate the shaft winding engine but after heart attack he had to be taken off the job. He was a small, stocky fellow, always jovial. He worked on the level above me and so had a bird's eye view of whatever I was doing. His only means of heat up on that draughty sill was an old-fashioned, cast-iron stove with a pipe chimney coming out of the top. As well as providing warmth, the stove was also used to heat the tea. With an abundance of coal and air, at times it became white hot.

Geordie was full of devilish tricks which helped him to relieve the boredom. One of his favourites was to pick off the conveyor belt an old cutting pick, nut or bolt that had somehow been discarded into a coal

Prestwick colliery and screens, 1964.

tub and found its way to the surface, and place it on the hot stove until it got extremely hot. He would then put them back onto the conveyor belt and watch it descend to the lower level where I and four others were working. Because of the constant boredom of the job, as soon as you saw an object that was not coal or stone you immediately made a grab for it. Now imagine what happened when, completely unsuspecting, you eagerly grasped a piece of incredibly hot metal! After the initial shock, you would look up to the level above to see Geordie doubled up with laughter and tears running down his cheeks.

One of the former underground workers who was now working in the sheds was Michael K. Due to an accident at the coalface he had to have his left leg amputated, although this did not appear to hinder his movement in any way. I remember watching him after a shift, running for a bus that was approaching in the distance. Unfortunately for Michael, his leg dropped off causing him to roll over on the ground. Picking himself up, he gathered up his left leg, put it under his arm and hopped the rest of the way to catch the bus.

About once a month the colliery manager presented himself on the screens to carry out a routine inspection. At this time there was a special effort being made by all colliery personnel to try and produce a larger type of coal, which would sell for more money per ton. Just as the manager arrived at the screens Michael was feeding the stove with coal. The manager looked at Michael and said, 'I hope you're not putting large coal on that stove Michael.' 'Oh no,' said Michael, 'I'm breaking it up first.' The manager turned around and walked away, shaking his head in disbelief, muttering 'idiot, bloody idiot!'

After my first day at work I arrived home to find that Mam had a lovely hot bath waiting for me. There were no pithead baths at that time; they were built two years later in 1955. We were fortunate living at the terrace, as all 12 houses had their own 'proper' bath fitted in the scullery, unlike the people down the road in the pit cottages who were forced to use a tin bath. They bathed in front of a large open fire in winter and out in the backyard in the summer. In one family, the father and five sons, who all worked at the colliery, used a tin bath for bathing. Imagine the difficulties that faced the mother, who not only had to provide a constant stream of hot water, but also had to cook on the open fire at the same time as there was no gas or electricity.

After I'd had a bath I was sitting having dinner when Mam said that it might not be necessary for me to have a bath every day as I wasn't all that dirty. However, I insisted that I should like to have one. The next day, in order to impress upon Mam the need for me to have a daily bath, at every opportunity during the shift I would rub my brow, touch my cheek or scratch my nose with my dirty hands. When I arrived home, Mam took one look at me and erupted. She screamed with laughter so long and hard that eventually she had trouble breathing. When I looked at myself in the mirror, I could see why. My face was as black as the ace of spades. I looked just like Al Jolson!

I received no pay after the first week of work because you had to have one week's pay 'lying on'. I got my first pay packet on the following Friday, it contained the princely sum of £2 and 16 shillings. I shall always remember that day. Mam was standing with a clean pinny on, waiting for me at the backyard gate. She ushered me into the house and I placed my pay packet on the kitchen table. 'There you are Mam' I beamed. She picked up the pay packet, put it to her lips and kissed it. Then she put her arms around me and hugged me until it almost hurt. She then started to sob and cry, but in a happy way. Later I was given ten shillings for pocket money. Words cannot express my satisfaction.

I had been working on the screens for a few weeks when one day the machine that drove the screening plant broke down. Tommy P., self-appointed foreman/fitter, was the man in charge of oiling and greasing the mechanical parts of the machine in order to keep it running smoothly. It was crucial to keep the screens running because if the screening plant broke down all production at the colliery came to a standstill. I learned at an early age that we were all involved in the efficient running of the colliery and everyone was a link in the chain.

I watched Tommy as he climbed down the steel ladder to the engine house to examine the trouble. 'What's wrong?' I shouted. 'I can see the trouble lad,' he replied. 'I'll need a long stand from the blacksmith's. Pop along and get me one,' he said. Off I went, running down the steel staircase and across the pit yard to the blacksmith's. I arrived excited and out of breath 'The screens are standing,' I gasped, and I've been sent for a long stand.' 'All right lad, stand there and I'll see what I can do.' He was busy sharpening coal cutting picks in the furnace ready for the afternoon shift. I was mesmerised by his skill. 'How's your Mam?' he asked. 'Very well,' I replied. 'How long have you been working on the screens?' 'Not long,' I said. He then went on to ask about different members of the family, all the time sharpening more and more picks. 'What about the long stand for the screens?' I eventually asked. He replied with a chuckle, 'Don't you think you've been standing there for long enough lad?' Long stand, standing there, the penny eventually dropped. I was furious. 'Give my regards to your Mam,' the blacksmith shouted as I ran back to the screening plant. I soon noticed that the screening plant was working normally and old Tommy and the other 'screeners' were all outside on the gantry, leaning on the hand rails, laughing their heads off at me for falling for such a simple prank.

Next day I managed to get my own back. I sneaked into the bike shed and let both the tyres down on Tommy's bike. At four o'clock, when I passed the cycle shed on the way home, Tommy was furiously pumping up his tyres. 'Have you got a puncture?' I enquired mischievously. 'I'll puncture you, you young bugger, when I get hold of you,' he shouted. Off I ran home to tell Mam. I shouldn't have, although she found it funny I still got a clip round the ear. Tommy never asked for me a 'long stand' again and I never let down his tyres.

There were two coal seams worked at the colliery – the Busty seam and the Brockwell seam. The Busty seam was thin and low, its height averaged about 27 inches, but sometimes it was lower than 20 inches. This seam produced the cleanest coal, with very little ash content and a high calorific value. The Brockwell seam, on the other hand, produced coal with a very high ash content and little calorific value; its height averaged 36 to 40 inches.

The two seams were worked on opposite shifts, for example the Brockwell on days and the Busty on nights. This alternated weekly. When the Busty seam was being worked during the day, there was very little for me to do as the coal was fairly 'clean' and there were hardly any stones mixed in with it.

Next to the screen buildings was the 'land sale' site where the private contractors would arrive with their wagons and hand fill one-hundredweight bags of coal onto the back of their lorries. The job entailed filling coals, with a hand shovel, into a scoop that held one-hundredweight, and then putting the coal into hessian bags. To alleviate the boredom of the screens, I would fill bags of coal for the contractors. They gave me ten shillings. However, all good things come to an end. When the yard foreman, caught me he gave me a good ticking off and said that if he ever caught me again, he would send me to the manager.

I worked on the screens for six months. What I remember most, apart from the humour of the men, was the boredom, the noise, the dust, and the cold. Someone had halved the length of the shed by hanging canvas sheeting from the roof. The idea was to save some of the heat that was escaping from the stove but it had no effect whatsoever. In the winter months we took turns sitting next to the hot stove, one side of your body would be nice and warm, while the other side was clay cold.

Light in the building was also very poor as most of the glass windows had been broken and replaced with wood or cardboard. The noise came from several sources. The loudest noise was coming from the screening plant itself, which gave off a methodical banging sound. Added to this, you had the noise of the squeaking rollers crying out for oil and the sound of coal falling from the conveyor belt onto the screening plant, or jigger as it was commonly known. The roof and sides of the building were made of corrugated tin sheeting. On windy days loose tin sheeting would bang and rattle together, making the most horrendous clatter. There was also the constant vibration caused by the jerking action of the jigger.

On Saturday mornings I worked in the timber yard unloading timber from the rail wagons and stacking it neatly into square piles. This was a great relief from the job on the screens and I got paid time and a half because it was considered as overtime.

It was on a Saturday morning that I was first taken down the mine. Bill T. and I were busy stacking timber in the timber yard when Bill M., an underground worker, came up to me and said, 'How would you like to go down the pit?' I could hardly believe my ears. Go down the pit! I was shaking with excitement. 'Come on,' he said 'Both of you follow me.'

The timber yard was just a few seconds away from the shaft. Jack W. was the winding engine man and he operated the engine that hauled the cages up and down the shaft.

He was standing on a platform outside the winding engine house when Bill M. shouted up to him, 'Jack, we're takin' the young'uns doon so go canny.' We walked into the cage at ground level. Normally everyone had to descend from the level above, only the shaftsman got in at this level because he had to load the cage with materials and supplies of timber, and to examine the shaft's condition.

My cousin Jimmy was the onsetter. It was his job to put the full tubs of coal or stone into the cage at the bottom of the shaft and then signal the cage to the surface, or 'bank', as it is commonly known underground. The cage held only four people at a time and there was a notice to this effect displayed on the wooden fencing that surrounded the shaft. Everyone obeyed this rule as it would be impossible to get any more people in; the cage was a mere three-and-a-half feet square and five feet high.

There were two cages in the shaft. Each cage had its own rope and was separated from the other cage by steel runners that ran down the centre of the shaft. Both cages operated simultaneously, so when one cage was at the bottom of the shaft, the other one would be at the surface.

Getting into the cage for the first time is an experience I shall never forget. There was a space between the edge of the shaft and the floor of the cage. Looking down I could see a dull yellow light, beyond that there was a second light and the drop appeared to be unending. To get into the cage I had to step over this void, I was extremely nervous although I tried very hard not to show it. We all got in, Bill M., Bill T., myself and then cousin Jimmy. 'Hang on,' said Jimmy and then he signalled to the winding engine to lower away. 'Keep a tight hold,' said Bill M. jokingly, 'just in case the bottom drops out.' All of a sudden the cage dropped and then slowly it gathered speed. I closed my eyes for a few seconds and when I opened them there was a flash of light as we passed the first inset. This was the entrance to the Busty seam. There was then a very strong draught as the other cage passed us on its way to the surface. The cage slowed down and the floor seemed to be pushing my feet up to my knees.

The cage landed with a gentle thud and we had arrived at the bottom.

Jimmy reached out of the cage and pushed along the gate, which was suspended on rollers and moved freely. Stooping, we all moved out of the cage, one at a time. The electric light appeared to be dull at first but gradually your eyes got used to it. This was one of the few places in the entire mine that had electric lighting as Prestwick was a naked light pit. Everyone carried their own light, either hand-held or attached to a cloth cap. Most miners at that time used cloth caps instead of the protective helmet.

The lamps had two compartments, one for water and one for carbide. Water dripping onto the carbide gave off a highly flammable ethyne gas which, when ignited, produced our means of light. The length of the flame depended on the speed at which the water dropped on to the carbide, the faster the water dropped, the longer the flame and the brighter the light. Each man bought his own lamp and the carbide and was responsible for his own light.

The shaft and siding were L-shaped. After stepping from the cage you could move forward in an upright position, but turning left the height of the roof gradually dropped to an even four feet. The length of the siding was approximately 25 yards. The floor area of the shaft entrance was made from three-by-two-foot steel plates, all neatly joined together and very slippery underfoot. The walls were made of red brick that had once been whitewashed. One of the walls was a small blackboard with numbers chalked on it which, I learned later, represented the number of tubs that had been sent to the surface.

'Right lads,' said Bill M., 'Follow us.' We walked behind them, along the siding, in a stooped position without any light. 'Now we'll see what you're made of,' said Jimmy. At the end of the siding were two tubs filled to the brim with building bricks and each had a bag of cement on the top. There were two sets of miniature railway lines running parallel along the siding. The two eventually joined together to form a single track; this was known as the crossing. It was exactly like a railway siding but in miniature. 'Right now, start pushing,' said Jimmy. The two of us started to push one of the tubs into complete darkness. We pushed it for about 50 yards when Jimmy called to us to stop. Both he and Bill M. had followed behind but by now they both had their lamps fitted to their caps, providing at least some light. 'Keep back out of the road,' said Bill. They then proceeded to manhandle the tub, lifting it off the track. I noticed in the dimness that we were at a four-way junction and we had to push the tub along the track to the right.

Once they had got the tub onto the right track, we had to push it up an incline. We eventually arrived at the end of the track. Here was an enormous cave with large lumps of rock protruding from the floor to the roof, just like a small mountain. Part of the cave contained two brick walls that had been partially built, obviously this is where the bricks were required. The structure was intended to house the new haulage machinery. Prestwick was in the process of changing the haulage system and driving a new tunnel which would eventually shorten the journey from the shaft to the coalface.

The cave was littered with huge rocks. I wondered how on earth anyone would move them. They were at least seven or eight times the size of the coal tubs. Later I was to discover that the large rocks had several short holes drilled into them which were filled with an explosive powder and detonator with a fuse wire attached to it. The explosives shattered the rocks into much smaller, manageable stores. Stones that were still too big to handle would eventually be broken down by hand. This was done by men using a seven- or 14-pound mallet, pounding the stones as hard as they could. Breaking the stones by hand could be made much easier if you hit them in just the right spot. This is where experience and common sense made the job much easier.

I was taught these basic skills by Bob Y. He was sitting on an upturned bucket in the middle of the cave mending his trousers with a needle and thread. 'Where've you been?' he said, laughing. 'We've been waiting all morning for the bricks haven't we Mat?' In the dimness I could see Mat C., the colliery bricklayer, pointing at the wall that had just been built. 'These two young buggers will never make pitmen,' he said. 'They're far too slow.'

We emptied out the bricks and cement and took the tub back to the shaft siding. We then returned to the cave with the second tub of bricks and cement. By this time we were both sweating and breathing heavily. When we were at the shaft siding you could feel the cold air being sucked down the mine. But at the site of the new hauler house there was a horrible musty smell due to a lack of ventilation. Also, the new workings had just holed into the old workings and released foul air. This situation would never exist in modern mines as an auxiliary electric fan would be fitted to the workings to provide 'fresh' air.

The two of us sat down to cool off and watched Bob breaking up the large stones. He seemed to be using very little effort and broke the stones up with apparent ease. 'Here, you have a go,' he said, throwing the fourteen pound mallet towards me. He pointed to a large stone, 'Break that one up.' I picked up the mallet, raised it above my head and hit the stone as hard as I could.

Nothing happened, the stone remained the same shape and size. I did this half a dozen times, all to no avail. 'Give it to me,' he said taking hold of the mallet. He proceeded to smash up the stone, using a lot less effort than I had employed. Sometimes he would turn the stone into a different position before striking it. 'Why do you do that?' I asked. He explained that breaking stones could be made easier by studying the faces and grain of the stone. 'Use the outside edge of the mallet,' he said, 'this helps to act as a chisel and splits the stone.' I tried again and this time had some success.

Bob was what was known as a 'company man', never involved in production but whose skill and mining knowledge were second to none. He would drive drifts, sink staples and do numerous skilled jobs away from the coalface. He was the complete miner.

'Howay back to bank,' said Jimmy. We followed him to the bottom of the shaft and got into the cage. We were then hauled slowly up to the surface. Arriving at the surface the first thing that struck me was the brilliance of the light. I had to shield my eyes as the light was actually hurting them. It took several seconds before I became accustomed to the dazzling light above ground.

We had been underground two hours and by now it was almost 11 o'clock. Returning to the timber yard we continued to unload the wagon. Then we were spotted. 'Where the bloody hell have you two idiots been?' 'Down the pit,' I replied. Apparently we had not been authorised to go. It was just as well that nothing had happened to us otherwise all hell would probably have been let loose!

Shortly after that first underground experience, Bill T. and I were summoned to the under-manager's office. We had to report to the Safety Officer, who was also the Training Officer. 'Right lads,' he said, 'I'm sending the pair of you to Weetslade next Monday to do your basic underground training. You'll be there for 16 weeks.' Weetslade was a colliery in the south of Northumberland where all young mining entrants were sent to do their training. There was no transport provided and the colliery was about six miles away. But as we both had bicycles, this presented no problem.

I couldn't wait for Monday to come around. The thoughts of going underground at Weetslade got me really excited. It never occurred to me that I might be entering a very dangerous environment, let alone the fact that several men had beep killed there in an explosion a few years earlier. Unlike Prestwick, Weetslade was a safety lamp mine and no naked lights or flames were allowed underground. This was because the workings were subject to methane gas (commonly known as firedamp).

Weetslade was a deeper mine than Prestwick and much larger, it employed four times as many men. A mock training face, or 'gallery', was set up to facilitate the training of new entrants. However, only part of our training was carried out underground. Most of it was done at the surface, in classrooms, discussing theory, practice and first aid. I didn't enjoy this bit at all. For me, it was too much like school and, stupidly, I considered it a big waste of time.

When underground at the training face we were shown how to build a wood-chock support. We then had to build one ourselves, knock it down and build another one. As you can imagine, this became quite boring. Quite near to the shaft was the main pumping station. All the water was pumped to this spot before being sent up, via the shaft, to the surface. What impressed me most of all was how clean the place was. It was spotless. The brick walls were whitewashed, the pumping machinery painted and all the brass was polished and shining. The pump attendant allowed no one into the building other than those persons appointed by the manager. He only allowed us in when the supervisor was present and we were instructed not to touch anything.

Part of our training was to learn about the wire rope haulage system. During this training, I remember having to travel what seemed like miles, mostly in a stooped position which made it extremely uncomfortable. There was also a dreadful musty smell and the temperature was quite warm. This was because we were travelling in the return airways which meant that the air had already travelled down the intake shaft, along the main roadway to the face, passing the electric motors and fans and picked up heat from the strata as it floated passed us on the way to the surface.

Having to travel in such conditions meant that we frequently had to stop for a breather. It was during one of these rests that I first tried tobacco. The habit was quite common in those days. I was offered a 'chew' by the supervisor and, at first, I declined. But after some persuasion I accepted. I placed a plug of tobacco in my mouth and started to chew. After a short while my mouth became really hot and I wanted to spit out the tobacco, but instead of spitting it out, I swallowed it. Within a few minutes I became ill and was soon very sick. To this day I've never had another chew of tobacco. I think it's a disgusting habit but some miners found it very pleasant. I have known some men who could actually gauge the time of day by the amount of tobacco they had chewed and the amount they had left.

Weetslade was a 'gassy' pit and so no chances could be taken with smokers. As we were juveniles we were probably regarded as an obvious risk so, at the beginning of every shift we were searched for contraband by the instructors and then again, just before entering the cage, by the banksman.

I didn't enjoy my 16-week basic training course. Most of the training became boring and very repetitive and I was very keen to get back to Prestwick and start on a proper underground job! My main objective was to emulate the high performance of my two brothers.

2 Life at Prestwick colliery

In 1954 Prestwick colliery operated an eight-hour, three-shift cycle. The shifts were the fore-shift, starting at 11.30pm; the back-shift, starting at 7.00am; and the night-shift, which started at 2.00pm. Modern coastal pits worked a four shift cycle due to the ever-increasing distances that had to be travelled to get to the coalface. There was a lot of confusion over the names of the shifts. For example, some men call the fore shift the night shift while others will call it the day shift. Confused? Just to add to the problem, Westoe Colliery worked a seven-shift system which alternated every three months!

There were three onsetters working the shaft at Prestwick; Danny F., my cousin Jimmy and Mr A. It was their job to send up the full tubs of coal to the surface and receive the empties, or 'chummings', that were returned. Each man worked one of the three shifts. Danny and Jimmy alternated weekly between the fore-shift and the back-shift while Mr A. did permanent night-shift. This was because he was approaching retirement age and, as very little production took place during the night-shift in those days, his job wasn't as hectic and the pace was much slower.

As I was still only 15 I wasn't allowed to work the fore-shift or the night-shift, so for three months I worked permanent back-shift. On alternate weeks I would work with Danny and then Jimmy, and occasionally with Mr A.

Mr A. had two sons; both were exceptional football players. In fact, Bobby turned a full-time professional with Bristol Rovers and Ronnie played for Newcastle Reserves. Mr A. was extremely proud of them, and rightly so. I can remember that he started wearing gloves for work –

most unusual at the time. When I asked him why, he replied, 'I've been invited down to Bristol for the weekend and I may have to go into the Directors' box. You never know who I might have to shake hands with.'

Mr A. was a great chapel man who never swore and was always polite. In fact he was a really nice old man. He was involved in the first accident that I had underground. It was my job to lower the set of full tubs that had been sent from the coalface into the shaft siding. To do this I had to detach the haulage rope from the tubs while the tubs were still moving. I had to be nimble and alert the whole time, speed and precision were important. However, to cut a long story short, the set of tubs derailed and, before I could detach the steel haulage rope, the first tub ran over my right foot, crushing the protective steel toe cap that covered my toes.

The set of tubs came to a stop and Mr A. came rushing towards me. I was lying on my back holding my right foot in the air. The pain was unbearable. However, as soon as I got my boot off I felt an instant relief. Mr A., on the other hand, stood open-mouthed and very pale, with a look of fear on his face. He was afraid that I'd broken my foot. I could sense his relief when, after a careful inspection, he realised that I had only been slightly bruised. The steel toe cap had certainly done its job. If I had not been wearing those protective boots I would almost certainly have lost my foot.

Mr A. took off the crushed toe cap before I put the boot back on. I told no one of the accident in case Mr A. got into trouble, as I was under his supervision at the time. Later that day when Mam was cleaning my boots she enquired about the toe cap. I told her that it had somehow just worked loose and eventually dropped off.

For most of my time as a shaft lad I worked with Danny – what a character he was! He was a portly man who always walked with style and he was a born comedian. At times he was very officious about his job. He certainly was a law unto himself. If anyone wanted to get to the surface they had to wait until Danny allowed it. Even the colliery manager could not get to the surface until Danny said so. He firmly believed that you should not stop production for anyone.

Every morning at seven o'clock the under-manager and the overman would arrive at the bottom of the shaft to check the back-shift as they emerged, four at a time, from the cage. This 'winding time' took approximately ten to 15 minutes.

The under-manager's method of recording and deploying the men was very crude. He was only interested in two types of workers, putters and coal fillers. He recognised them by the clothes they wore, for example, a filler would wear long trousers and leather knee pads, and a putter wore short trousers and no pads. On the wall at the bottom of the shaft was a blackboard where the overman would mark a cross for a filler and a dash for a putter; the rest of the workmen were not recorded.

Quite often, Danny would tell a joke just before the cage reached the bottom, deliberately distracting the managers. When all the men had arrived, the under-manager and the overman would be scratching their heads in confusion, not knowing how many men were doing what job. Often they would have to consult Danny, who kept a mental note of every man that he'd seen.

After a few minutes' deliberation the under-manager and the overman were ready to return to the surface but before Danny signalled the cage away he would tell a few more jokes. 'Ya kna Bill,' he would say to the under-manager, 'a loove work. A love it that much, a could lie doon next to it and watch it all day!' 'Danny, if yu divn't get me to bank, al swing for yu laddy!' 'Ya ganna swing for us now Bill,' replied Danny. 'Ta ta.' And then he'd signal the cage to the surface.

I can still picture under-manager and the overman standing at the bottom of the shaft. The under-manager would have on an old raincoat covering most of his clothes. He wore a flat cloth cap, always back-to-front, and he carried a hand-held carbide lamp with a large brass reflector shield, reflecting the naked flame and giving off quite a bright light. The overman wore a long-sleeved waistcoat, plus-four trousers and blue, knee-length socks. His black polished helmet matched his polished knee pads and boots. He carried a notched yard stick, which was used as a walking stick and an instrument to measure with.

In those days the youths always had to address their seniors as 'Mr' as a sign of respect. If Mam overhead me calling the under-managers or overmen by their Christian names I would get a good telling off. Gradually I got to know all the men and what jobs they did. I became so good at this that I took over the recording for the under-manager, much to his relief. Two years later, he retired and came to live in the terrace. Most days, after I'd finished my tea, I would go and sit with him at the top of his garden path and tell him what had been going on at work that day. Even though he had retired, he was still very keen to hear about the pit. Sadly, he died of a heart attack only a few months after retiring. I felt really sorry for him; he'd worked hard all his life and then was unable to enjoy his years in retirement.

I remember telling the under-manager when it was my 16th birthday, (it fell on a Friday). 'I'm 16 now, so can I work the fore-shift on Monday?' He looked at me in astonishment, and then his chubby red face started beaming. 'Thow's just the lad I've been looking for. Start Sunday night with Danny. That's grand, just grand,' he said.

Over the weekend I was so excited, I couldn't wait for Sunday evening to come around. I remember thinking that working during the night would leave me all day free to do whatever I chose. How wrong I was. By 4am I was absolutely exhausted, my head throbbed, I had a constant thirst, my legs and arms ached and they felt as if they were on fire.

My job as a shaft lad was, first of all, to escort the full set of tubs, that had been received from the coalface into the shaft siding. You did this by placing steel dregs (short steel bars) into the wheels of the tubs and gradually bringing the set to a standstill. You then changed over the steel haulage rope from the full set onto the empty set. The haulage operator would set his engine in motion and pull the empties out of the shaft siding, lowering them down an inclined tunnel away from the shaft and nearer to the coalface.

Meanwhile, Danny would have placed the first full tub into the empty cage and sent it to the surface. It was now my job to keep Danny supplied with full tubs while, at the same time, receiving the empties that had been sent down from the surface. Each tub, full and empty, had to be pushed by hand along the shaft siding, a distance of 25 yards, and then coupled together. On an average shift, there would be about 18 sets of tubs, each set containing 18 tubs, making a total of approximately 300 tubs. Every tub had to be coupled and uncoupled, which meant bending 600 times during one shift, as well as travelling up and down the shaft siding with each tub. Having had no sleep at all on the evening before starting work, the excitement of working through the night quickly lost its appeal.

An eight-hour shift was operating at the time and, during the shift, we were allowed a 30-minute break to have our bait. (Workers at, or near to, the coalface were allowed only 20 minutes). The three of us, Danny, the engine operator and I, would have our bait in the engine house, which was half way along the shaft siding. It was out of the main air stream and used to get quite warm due to the heat coming from the electric engine.

My bait consisted of six sandwiches – two meat, two cheese, and always two jam, or 'pitman's ham', as we used to call it. Mam brought me a small thermos flask for my tea and I also carried a tin bottle of water. Somehow, jam always tasted much sweeter underground. I can remember as a boy of seven, in 1945 just after the war, waiting by the railway line for Dad to come home from work – he always saved me a jam sandwich. In those days bread was rationed and so it certainly was a treat.

While I was working at the shaft, the new tunnel that shortened the distance from the shaft to the coalface had been completed, the large new engine house was ready and a brand new hauler had been installed.

The haulerman couldn't wait to get his hands on it. He was a small, smart, meticulous man who never broke into a sweat and never seemed to get himself dirty. After a full shift at work he looked as clean and tidy as he had been when he arrived at the pit.

He looked after that new hauler like a mother would care for her first-born baby. He polished it, painted it, oiled it, and dusted it. It was spotless. He whitewashed the walls and even painted some of the support girders.

If you wanted to know the time underground you had to ask the haulerman as he was the only person at the shaft who wore a watch. He kept it in his trouser pocket underneath his overalls and so every time you asked him the time he would practically undress himself to get at his watch, yet it never occurred to him to put it in a different pocket! Danny was always asking him the time just for sheer devilment. The haulerman never lost his cool, but everything became 'you little blighter.' He never ever swore. His main hobby was cycling and every weekend he and his wife cycled all over the countryside on a tandem.

During the fore-shift, every morning at six o'clock on the dot, the phone on the wall at the bottom of the shaft would ring. It would be the under-manager to find out how many tubs of coal had been sent to the surface during the shift. I would check the total on the small blackboard beside the phone and give him the answer. If Danny answered the phone before me he would often give him a fictitious total, making him believe the pit had been idle for most of the shift. Then, when the under-manager almost believed him, he would tell him the right answer. The under-manager was always going to sack Danny!

Ponies were last worked underground at Prestwick in the 1930s. However, the stables were still there in my time, just around the corner from the shaft bottom in a tunnel that was rarely used, but was, in fact, the main return roadway to the second, or upcast, shaft. I worked at the downcast shaft. A large electric fan on the surface sucked fresh air into the downcast shaft, all over the coalface workings, and back to the surface via the upcast shaft.

There was a terrible incident at the end of the 19th century at the New Hartley colliery in Northumberland. A large wooden beam collapsed, completely blocking off the only shaft at the mine. Over 200 men lost their lives. Since that accident a law was passed which stated that every mine must have a second exit.

When I was shown the second shaft I also discovered the stables. As the cage in the shaft was so small I wondered how on earth they managed to get the ponies underground. My Uncle Matty told me that they used to sling them with a special harness attached to the underside of the cage and gently lower them to the bottom. I suppose the same method was used for returning them to the surface.

The reason for there being no ponies in my time was simple. The main roadway from the shaft to the coalface had become so low it was impossible to get the ponies in or out of the mine. The last pony to work down the mine at Prestwick was kept, fed and watered, at the coalface (or inbye, as we called it) because it was impossible to return it to the surface. When the manager discovered this he got so mad that he had the pony tied to the end of a set of tubs and dragged out from the face workings to the shaft, where it was then raised to the surface.

As a shaft lad, I frequently rode up and down from the Brockwell seam to the Busty seam, and once I was accustomed to this procedure my fear of travelling in the cage soon vanished. Shortly after I'd started at the shaft, there was an incident involving four men who were about to start their afternoon shift. They entered the cage at the surface ready to descend. Normally, the banksman would pull a lever which released four iron bars ('keps') that supported the underside of the cage as it came to rest. (If, for example, the winching rope was to snap while the cage was at the surface, these 'keps' would prevent the cage from plunging down the shaft). On this occasion the banksman signalled to the haulerman to lower the cage but had forgotten to release the 'keps'. The winching rope was released, but because the 'keps' were still in place the cage was prevented from descending into the shaft. As a result, the rope coiled on top of the cage. When the banksman realised that he had forgotten to release the 'keps', he panicked and operated the lever, thus removing the supports from underneath the cage. The cage plunged 20 feet before taking up the loose rope. So incensed and shocked was one of the workmen that he refused to go underground for several weeks. The other three grumbled and swore at the banksman for being so irresponsible, but eventually went underground and carried on with the shift as it nothing had happened.

On rare occasions the colliery manager would come down the pit, but he never ventured further than the shaft siding. Sometimes he would check on the progress of the new engine house. There was a large crack in the whitewashed wall which ran from the floor to the ceiling of the existing engine house. He would often measure the width of this crack to see if it was getting bigger. I asked him why he did this and he said it was just out of curiosity because when the new hauler house had been completed, the existing hauler house would be of no use.

He asked Danny how I was managing the job. 'Best shaft lad I've ever had,' said Danny. 'Well, if you're half as good as your Dad and your two brothers, you'll do.' Listening to conversations and by talking to the men, I soon discovered that both Cyril and Reg held records for filling the greatest number of coal tubs in a shift, and in a week. However Cyril had to give up coal filling because of cartilage trouble in his knees. Before giving up this job he had attended weekend courses and night classes to qualify for a Deputy's and Shot-firing Certificate. This meant he could go on to take charge of a whole district, instead of spending the whole shift on his knees shovelling coal.

At the beginning of every shift, before entering the cage, the coal fillers would collect bunches of tokens from the weigh cabin on the surface. These metal tokens were about 12 inches long and attached to a hemp rope, which was then tied to the man's belt. As the fillers walked from the shaft to the coalface, usually a distance of about two miles, you could hear a continuous 'jingle jangle' sound as the tokens dangled from the men's waists. Reg, being one of the top fillers, would carry as many as 70 tokens at a time plus a canister of explosives, a water bottle, his bait and a tin of carbide to replenish his lamp. I often wondered whether I would be able to fill as many tubs as our Reg and carry on the good name of the Grahams.

Once the new roadway and haulage system was completed and in operation, production at the Brockwell seam could be increased. The new roadway had shortened the distance from the shaft to the coalface, as well as increasing the size of the tunnel. The new haulage system meant that the number of tubs in a set could be increased from 18 to 25.

I was sent away from the shaft, to work at a place known as the 'inbye' landing. This was where empty tubs were received and prepared to be sent further 'inbye' towards the coalface and full tubs were waiting to be sent to the shaft. My job, as landing lad, was to change the steel rope from the set of empty tubs and then couple it onto a set of full tubs. I would then signal to the haulerman to pull the set of full tubs 'outbye' towards the shaft.

The signalling system was simple and straightforward. Pressing a brass button on the wall of the engine house rang a bell telling the operator to put his engine in motion. One ring meant stop, two rings meant lower and three rings meant haul the set to the shaft.

The 'landing' was four feet high (just over tub height), eight feet wide and 90 feet long. It was like a miniature railway station with two tracks running parallel to each other for 90 feet and then crossing together to form a single track. Each end of the landing had a dim electric light so I still needed a cap lamp to travel from one end to the other.

Due to the height of the tunnel I had to walk in a stooped position with an ape-like action. Working in these cramped conditions all shift took some getting used to, but I was able to take a rest in between sets. I also had the hauler operator for company.

Herby R. was one of these 'hauler hands'. He was a bachelor in his late forties who was small in stature and always slouched. He was forever tripping himself up. Herby was simple minded but very kind. He was always eating sweets and had an extremely annoying habit of making a loud sucking noise with each one he ate.

At about this time, the old colliery manager retired and a new manager, Mr Rothery, took over. The new manager was a strict disciplinarian and a very religious man. He had high standards of hygiene and it was he who introduced toilets underground. One of these toilets, a chemical bucket placed in a small, white-washed brick building, was situated right where Herby worked and it was his job to keep it clean. Every Friday he would take the bucket to the surface, empty out the contents and fill it with fresh chemicals.

On one occasion, as Herby was ascending to the surface with the bucket, the cage came to a sudden stop. The lid from the bucket had not been properly secured and flew off as the cage jolted to a standstill. Poor Herby was covered from head to foot with the contents. Herby stank. The cage stank. And even the shaft stank. Poor Herby could only grumble at his misfortune.

Not long after that incident, however, Herby got the last laugh. There's a saying 'shit for luck', and it certainly worked in Herby's case for he won £5,500 on the pools. In 1955, that was a lot of money. After receiving the cheque Herby brought it to work to show his workmates. Standing outside the pay office, I asked him what he was going to do with the pay cheque while he went underground. 'Am not gannin doon this afternoon,' said Herby, 'a've got mesell a sick note.' In those days if you missed a shift through ill health, you had to get a sick note from your doctor so that you could still receive your five-day week bonus, which was about one-sixth of your wages.

Not long after winning the pools Herby had another stroke of luck. Arriving for work on a Saturday morning, I found him standing on the heapstead waiting to go down the mine. As Herby seldom worked overtime, I asked him what he was doing. 'A've lost me pay, John,' he said disgruntedly. 'A just divint kna what a've done with it. Mebbe a've left it doon the pit,' he said. Normally on a Friday, Herby would collect his pay in the morning and take it down to work with him. His pay, in those days, would be about £8. 'I'll help you look for it,' I said to him.

We traced his route underground to where he had been working the Friday afternoon, but we couldn't find his pay anywhere. Herby went back to the surface and I went to work. On Monday afternoon, at the end of my shift and the beginning of Herby's, I asked him if he'd found his pay packet. He grinned at me sheepishly. 'Yes a fund it. It was in the farmer's field beside the bus stop.' On the Saturday morning, while standing waiting for the bus, he remembered that on the previous evening he had climbed into the farmer's field and stolen a turnip to take home. Out of curiosity, he'd retraced his steps and lo and behold, lying there tucked neatly in a row of turnips was Herby's pay, safe and sound.

Being simple, Herby was looked after by the colliery overman, Bill Rothery, who was the 'Master Shifter'. He was the man who made the colliery 'tick'. It was his job to plan and organise most of the underground operations. He was a small man, not much taller than five feet, who always wore a red and white spotted handkerchief, plus-four trousers with knee-length pit stockings and boots, a long-sleeved waistcoat and a green pit helmet which he wore back to front with a peak covering his neck.

It was Bill Rothery who advised Herby what to do with his pools winnings. 'Put it in the building society and leave it there,' he said. 'And don't let anyone scrounge off you. When you want to get some money out, come and let me know first.' 'OK,' said Herby. And this is just what he did. To Herby, Bill Rothery was God.

Not long after, Herby went to see Bill Rothery. 'Bill,' said Herby, 'I wanna draw some money oot of the Building Society.' 'What the bloody hell for?' replied Bill. 'Am ganna buy a motor car,' said Herby. 'A motor car!' exclaimed Bill. 'What the bloody hell do you want a motor car for? You can't drive. You'll just kill yerself, or some poor innocent bugger.'

'The brother-in-law's ganna lorn us,' said Herby. 'He says I've gotta get £20 and buy an auld banger to lorn in.'

Bill Rothery, after much spluttering and swearing, finally gave Herby his permission to withdraw £20. And with the help of his brother-in-law, Herby bought an old banger. However, when they came to drive it, it wouldn't start. The brother-in-law, lifting up the bonnet and scratching his head in bewilderment, declared that the battery must be flat, upon which Herby replied, 'What shape should it be?'

I worked as a 'landing lad' for a short while before moving nearer the coalface to become what was known locally as the 'flatter'. The 'flat' was where the haulage system ended and, from this point, the tubs were uncoupled one at a time and manhandled to the coalface. The flat was a central point, similar to a landing, approximately 300 feet from the coalface. It was my job, again, to uncouple the set of empties and couple the set of full tubs as they were brought to the flat by the putters. Normally, nine putters were received at one flat.

The flat was similar to a landing and was made up of a double track, crossing at both ends to form a single track. It was approximately 90 feet in length, eight feet wide and five feet high. This was the place where the putters had their bait. At bait times you would sit on a wooden plank on the floor and lean against one of the wooden prop supports. I used a thermos flask to keep my tea hot, but most of the lads would heat up their tin cans of tea using a candle.

It was my job, every bait time, to re-heat the cans of tea about 15 minutes before our break. I removed the wick from the centre of a wax candle and cut it into two-inch lengths. I wrapped newspaper around the candle and placed it between two stones that supported the tin can. When lit it produced a large flame that heated up the tea. I would have as many as eight tin cans and candles to look after. Just before the men arrived with their bait, I would have to taste each can and put out the candles when the tea was hot enough. If the tea was allowed to boil, which was quite often the case, the tea stewed and tasted revolting.

The conversation at bait times usually revolved around two main subjects, sex and football. We sometimes talked about the union and, on rare occasions, politics. Most discussions were light hearted, very rarely serious. Bait time only lasted 20 minutes and often the lads were too exhausted to talk much, especially in the fore-shift when bait time would be 4am.

It was during bait time that I first tried to push an empty tub from the landing to the coalface. The easiest route was to go straight ahead via the roadway known as the mother or main-gateway. Gate is the term used underground to describe a tunnel or roadway. At the time the longwall gates were being worked. Longwall was the coalface, a continuous length of over 100 yards divided into sections approximately 11 yards long, giving each coal filler their own section of coalface and their own gate.

There were nine tunnels leading to the coalface. The main-gate was the central tunnel, with four tunnels running either side of it. Each of the tunnels running away from the face joined into a single tunnel known as a cross gate. Altogether, there were three roads leading from the flat, the main-gate and two cross-gates.

The coal seam was on a natural incline, rising from the left to the right. The tunnels to the right of the main-gate were referred to as the highside workings, and those to the left were the lowside workings. Each tunnel was numbered, one highside, two highside, etc, and the same applied to the lowside.

Pushing tubs underground for the first time was very frustrating because it was so easy for them to become derailed, or 'off the way.' It was much easier once you'd got used to the feel of the tub and the rails, especially at joints and turns. When you became derailed with an empty tub it wasn't so difficult to lift it back on, but with a full tub it was a different matter; sometimes it would take three men to replace it on the rails.

When I eventually reached the coalface (having been off the way six times), instead of gently allowing the tub to go over the end of the track, I pushed the tub right off the end giving my Uncle Ernie, who was working at the face, a real fright. (Uncle Ernie was our next door neighbour). Not only had the tub gone completely over the track, it had also knocked out some of the face supports, bringing down part of the roof. After getting over the shock, Uncle Ernie helped me to get the tub back onto the track and put back the supports.

Uncle Ernie wore a cotton vest buttoned at the neck, short knee-length trousers, a pair of safety boots and knee pads, but nothing on his head. His carbide lamp hung from a nail on one of the wooden prop supports. It gave off a very poor light making the place look dark and spooky.

'Seeing as you're that keen to get to the face,' said Uncle Ernie, 'Let's see what you're made of.' He threw me a large, round shovel and told me to 'get cracking.' I was to fill up the empty tub. There was a pile of loose coals which he had thrown from the face to the roadway. I filled the tub with these coals but I had to stoop as the tunnel was only five feet high. It was very hard work and I was pleased when the tub was full. I pushed the tub from the coalface back to the 'flat' but at the crossing I got 'off the way' again. Gordon T., one of the putters, gave me a hand to put it back on.

My first journey to the coalface could so easily have ended in a disaster and it is something that I shall never forget. I will never forget the experience of seeing the coalface for the first time.

After a couple of weeks I got used to the organisation and running of the 'flat', and the 'non-stop' pace. I was so keen to become a putter that I used to help Gordon T., who was putter to our Reg. Reg was the top coal filler at the time, and, due to the distance from the face to the flat in such low, narrow tunnels, it was impossible to keep him supplied with empty tubs. He was working at the farthest point from the flat, No.4 highside.

So, apart from doing my own work, I pushed empty tubs to the cross-gate tunnel to meet Gordon, who gave me full tubs. This almost

Putter pushing a tub to the coalface.

halved Gordon's journey and helped Reg to produce more tubs of coal. He was averaging 65 tubs per shift (26 tons of coal), and held the record for producing the most tons of coal in a week; over 147.

Every filler at the colliery who produced over 100 tons a week received a bonus of ten shillings from the manager. 'Filling' meant Reg was throwing 26 tons of coal a distance of eight to ten feet, six hours a day, five days a week.

On the lowside workings it was physically impossible to push a full tub of coal up to the inclined cross-gate tunnel. To overcome this problem a small electric winch was installed to pull the tubs of coal. This took an enormous amount of physical effort out of the job so that it was a pleasure to work on the lowside.

The highside workings struck fear into the hearts of the putters because of the sheer physical effort required and the distances that had to be travelled under almost inhumane conditions. The roadways became so narrow and low due to the constant pressure and continual advancement of the coalface, that quite often supports would have to be removed because there was not enough room for them!

Taking the first tub to the face after the weekend along some of these roads was usually very difficult. If you complained to the deputy about these conditions and the fact that you couldn't get past a certain wood support, he would present you with an axe and you would have to chip away at the prop or plank to make enough room to get by. Often some of the track would have to be re-laid due to floor heave.

Most of the roads would start at five feet high and six feet wide, but as the face advanced the width and height decreased because of the constant pressure from the strata above and below. These roads normally had a life of about 13 weeks, depending on the rate at which the face advanced. By the time the road was at the end of its life there would be very few supports left in it. The roadway became like a natural arch with only enough room for a tub to be squeezed through. The size of the road would often have diminished to three-and-a-half feet wide and approximately the same height.

I was still only 16 when I got the chance to become a putter. One of the older lads had had enough and left the colliery to join the army. Having had a little practice through helping Gordon, I knew what I was letting myself in for. At the back of my mind I wondered whether or not I would be able to manage it. I had plenty of self-confidence but I always worried about letting the family name down.

On my first full shift as a putter my coal filler was Uncle Ernie and he was working on the dreaded highside. But, luckily it was No.1 highside, which was nearest to the mother gate, and so easiest to work. Uncle Ernie wasn't one of the best fillers but he could still manage around 45 to 50 tubs a shift. As he was in his fifties this was quite an

EFFECT of CONVERSION PRESSURE on ROADWAY

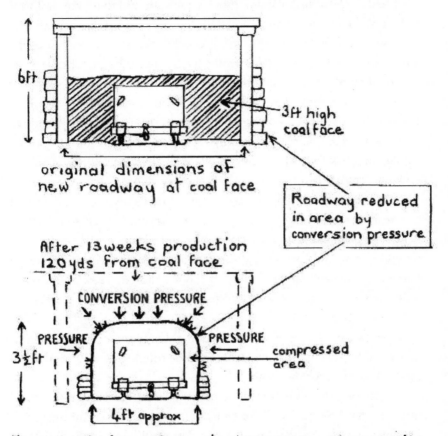

6ft

3ft high coalface

original dimensions of new roadway at coal face

Roadway reduced in area by conversion pressure

After 13 weeks production 120 yds from coal face

CONVERSION PRESSURE

PRESSURE

3½ft

PRESSURE

compressed area

4ft approx

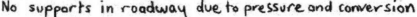

No supports in roadway due to pressure and conversion

Roadway has become a natural archway with only enough room for tubs to pass through.
All initial supports removed after becoming broken & useless.
Rail tracks buckle and have to be reset due to floor heave.

achievement.

I had supplied him with 47 tubs on my shift and that evening I was so sore and tired that I went to bed at 7pm and slept right through until 7am the next day. My legs, arms, back and neck ached so much I could have cried. But I couldn't tell anyone in case they thought I was lazy.

In all my years in mining there was never a job as cruel or soul-destroying as putting. It was both mentally and physically exhausting. I had seen men return to mining after being in the army and not last five minutes as a coal putter. It certainly separated the men from the boys.

As the weeks went by, each one of my vertebrae was bruised and scabbed through being scraped along the low ceilings. Try to imagine what it's like pushing tubs through a tunnel that's only three-and-a-half feet high, with your body at full stretch and trying to keep your back just below the height of the tub. Now and again I did cry. Some of the scabs on my back would have nearly healed when I would accidentally scrape my back along the ceiling, taking off the scab and more skin. But you didn't dare show any weakness for fear of ridicule. After all we were all in the same boat.

The pace of the job was so demanding. Every shift was a competition and a real hard slog. Everyone wanted to be top dog. It was no place for shirkers, cowards or the weak.

Ventilating the tunnels in those days was a problem and a very crude method was employed. Rolls of canvas were hung up like curtains at various points across the tunnel. We had to push our way through them on our journey to and from the coalface. If the conditions were wet the canvas doors become saturated and as you passed through them you got very wet and extremely dirty. The dust and grit really irritated our skin.

Due to the exhausting pace everyone used to sweat profusely and so very little clothing was worn. I wore only football shorts, a vest, knee-length woollen stockings, a pair of hob-nailed boots and a cloth cap which held my lamp. During the first hour of the shift the sweat literally poured off us and each man was surrounded by his own cloud of steam.

The sweat used to sting the wounds on our backs because of the natural salt it contained.

Another common injury was on the shin bone. A full tub of coal coming down an incline had to be controlled. This was done by inserting steel dregs into the wheels of the tub causing the tubs to skid along the track. When this happened our legs occasionally slid underneath the tub catching on the steel axle. As there is very little flesh on your shins the skin was nearly always scabbed and took ages to heal. Hand and finger injuries were also very common.

Speed was essential when hand putting. The pace was usually dictated by the putter working in the first tunnel on the highside. The distance we had to travel from the coalface to the landing varied from 80 yards to 120 yards. On an average shift we would travel five or six miles in these low workings, as well as the three mile journey to and from the shaft.

The average thickness of the Brockwell seam was around three feet. The seam would be undercut to a depth of four-and-a-half feet, then drilled and charged with explosives before being blasted. This would normally be done before the fillers arrived at the face. About 30 tubs of coal could be filled straight from the face to the tub but the rest had to be thrown or 'casted' nearer to the tub. This meant that the fillers had to shovel the coals twice.

On occasions when a putter reached the face only to find that the tub was still empty, he would either slump down at the side of the tub and wait until the filler had filled it, or he would fill it himself. This enabled the filler to cast out more coals from the face to the roadway. It was illegal for a putter to fill coals if he had not been properly trained, but no one took any notice of this as the putters and fillers were paid by the amount of coal produced and we would do everything we could to produce as much coal as possible.

As the shift progressed, the fillers who kept their tubs constantly full would dictate the pace of their putter. This is where confusion arose and accidents started to happen. If a putter was late in coming to the flat, the rest of the putters would start on their inwards journey. The only warning we had about oncoming tubs was the sound made by the tubs running on the track. We would then shout ourselves hoarse if we heard another tub coming.

Very often three or four putters had to go back to the flat with their empty tubs to allow the late putter access to the flat. This is when tempers were lost and a few punches would be thrown. Eventually all would be forgiven and the cycle would resume.

Becoming derailed was quite common because of floor heave which distorted the track. I can remember once being derailed and finding it impossible to lift one end of the tub back onto the track because the tunnel was so small that I couldn't get past the tub. I had to crawl back along the roadway to the coalface, go down the face to the next roadway and travel down the adjacent roadway, eventually getting to the other side of my tub.

Sometimes the gradient on the highside was so severe that it was physically impossible for one man to push a tub by himself. We had to ask the flat lad to give us a hand to push the tub up the steepest part of the gradient. This also helped to break a new lad in and harden him to the job of putting. Only on very rare occasions would the management allow two men to push one tub because it meant having to take men away from development work. There was never any spare labour.

As a 16-year-old lad, I would be competing with men in their twenties. At first I found it very difficult to keen up with them, but I gritted my teeth and just kept going. Pushing a tub out of a flat was easy, it was when I started up the gradient (cross-gate) that it became hard going. Part of the road was so steep, that I'd be pushing the tub with my arms, shoulders, and head, often having to use one hand to pull myself along using the wooden supports, or even the rail track. Once I arrived at my tunnel, the ground was almost level making the job much easier. Travelling along this part of the roadway, I could get my breath back and

Loading coal into a tub.

take a breather while pushing the tub forward.

When I had almost reached the coalface I placed the tub in a small siding and then walked to the end of the roadway to reach the face itself. The full tubs would be standing slightly tipped, with two wheels over the edge of the track. This made it easier to fill the tub from a kneeling position. Crouching with my back to the tub, one hand on the wood buffer and the other hand between my legs holding the coupling links, I heaved and pushed with my back to lift the tub slowly onto the track. Still pushing with my back, my weight firmly against the tub, I had to turn around while keeping the tub moving. Once in position, I placed both hands on the tub handles and used the wood sleepers of the track as foot holds. I would push the tub past the small siding and leave it standing while I took the empty one to the face and lowered it gently over the edge of the track. I then went back to the full tub and started on the journey to the flat.

At the inclined cross-gate it was physically impossible to control the tub down the incline without assistance. So, while slowly negotiating the tub around the turn I inserted a steel dreg into one of the rear wheels giving me much more control. At the bottom of the incline I arrived back at the flat. I repeated this cycle again and again and again. Each trip took about five minutes, ten or 12 times an hour, six hours a shift. Much depended on each putter, filler and the conditions of the coalface. If it had been blasted well the filler could work easily without having to pick or hack at the coalface.

The cross-gates were half the length of the coalface and would vary in distance between 40 and 50 yards, depending on the number of workings – there were usually four. Normally the district had nine workings altogether, four high, four low, and the mother gate. Every three months the fillers' names would be put into a hat and drawn out to determine which section they would work on for the next three months. It was a very fair system of allocating positions. Each place was known as a 'cavil', if it was a bad 'cavil' you were stuck with it until the next 'cavilling' day. The same system applied to the putters.

When I first started work, each seam had its own separate cavil, but through time the NUM had this changed. Cavils were drawn for the whole pit, against the management's wishes. This was much fairer because different rates of pay applied to the different seams.

Every quarter the cavils would be drawn in the under-manager's office at the surface. It was officiated by a Union representative and Bill Rothery, the colliery overman. It was a time of much excitement and expectation. Having been a spare putter for several weeks now, I automatically thought that this time I would be cavilled and get my own gate to work.

The cavilling list was placed in Percy E.'s cabin on the heapstead next to the shaft. I scanned the list looking for my name but it wasn't there – there were plenty of Grahams on the list, but not John. I was almost choked with disappointment and anger. I couldn't believe that I'd not been cavilled. Some of the older men, realising my disappointment, suggested that I go and see Bill Rothery and ask him why. However, he couldn't be contacted that day as he was at a meeting.

The following day I met him underground. I was walking out of the mine after my shift as he was walking in. 'Can I have a word with you please,' I asked. 'Aye lad. What aboot?' 'Why I didn't get cavilled,' I said. 'Sit yourself doon here,' he said, motioning to the side of the track. 'I've been hearing damn good reports about you lad. But I still think you're a bit young to have a cavil.' 'But I've already worked every cavil as a spare,' I said. 'Aye, a kna. But supposing your Reg got cavilled there as well, could you manage to push 60 tubs a shift, every shift for a quarter?' he argued. 'Yes,' I said emphatically. Mr Rothery looked at me and grinned. 'Well,' he said, 'a thought mebbes it would brek ya heart, but divn' ye worry, I'll see that you're cavilled next quarter.'

Being only 16 I couldn't see his argument, but I had to accept it. He was as good as his word and the next quarter I was cavilled in the Brockwell seam at No. 1 on the lowside. My filler was Charlton T., the oldest filler at the colliery.

Charlton was a remarkable man. He was a bachelor approaching 70 years of age. He had obviously been a big, well-made man in his day but now the years were beginning to tell. He was always the first man at the colliery during that particular shift, he always got the first cage underground and was always the first to start work once at the coalface. He was a prime example of the fable about the tortoise and the hare – travelling underground he walked with the aid of an old pick axe handle and every step produced a grunt from him. Most men would catch him up and then overtake him. But because you were walking in a stooped position most of the time, every now and then you would stop for a breather. Not Charlton, he would plod on non-stop and always arrive at the face first.

Not only were his age and height against him in these terrible conditions. He also had to carry his carbide lamp, a five-pound canister of explosives, a bunch of 50 or more tokens, his tin water bottle and bait, and a hewing pick which he took to the surface every day to be sharpened by the blacksmith.

He was always smartly dressed and his clothes were probably too good to be worn underground. In fact, someone once remarked that Charlton was better dressed to go to work than most miners were in their Sunday best! He wore a tweed suit with matching waistcoat, hand-made hobnailed boots and a cloth cap, which he took off at the coalface and replaced with a black pit helmet. He had cord tied around his trouser legs just below the knee. He always carried his knee pads on his belt when travelling back and forward to the surface.

At the coalface he took off his jacket and waistcoat, exposing his thick neck and a buttoned-up vest. He was most remarkable in that, despite such dusty conditions, he always managed to keep himself fairly clean, not like some of the men who would come out looking as black as the ace of spades. And he didn't appear to perspire very much.

Watching the old man stumbling along in those dreadful conditions, you wondered how on earth he managed to fill a tub of coal. But once at the face, stripped off ready for action, he became a different person. He worked on his knees for the whole shift and he was extremely strong, and very agile. I never saw him stand to fill a tub of coal.

Charlton lived with his sister on a farm at a place called Black Callerton. It was about a mile across the fields to the south of the pit. He had worn a path across the fields on his daily journey back and forward to work. He didn't smoke or drink, but liked to gamble, especially on the horses. His weekends were taken up visiting race courses all over the country.

He was a very shrewd gambler and it was quite common for him to attend a race meeting without placing a bet. He would go to time a certain horse and only place a bet on it when he thought it was ready to win. He never had much time for women and thought that all they were after was his money. Rumour has it that he was a very rich man and had no need to work as he owned half the farm. Some of the workmen thought him stupid and greedy, but I found him to be a kind man and I respected him for his strong principles.

I remember waking up at about six o'clock one Saturday morning, I would have been about eight years old at the time, and heard the clip clop of a horse pulling a cart. I looked through my bedroom window to see Charlton sitting on the cart, steering the horse on his way to the pit. Years later I discovered that Charlton would rather seek his own coal than pay a shilling and sixpence to have it delivered.

A few years before I started work at Prestwick, Charlton had been trapped on the wrong side of a roof fall and was underground for almost 24 hours before the roadway could be cleared. I was curious to know what he thought and did when trapped underground. I was most surprised when he told me that he'd spent most of his time hewing coals at the face to help alleviate the boredom!

In 1950 he was awarded the British Empire Medal for services to mining and went to Buckingham Place to receive his medal from King George VI. He arrived home in the early hours of Monday morning. This meant missing a shift from work, but apparently he worked an extra shift on the Friday to make up for it!

For the few years that I knew Charlton, I cannot remember him ever being off work. Obviously, he couldn't keep pace with the younger men, some of whom would be half his age, yet he still managed to average around 40 tubs per shift. And because he never lost any work, his annual tonnage was often a good deal better than many of the younger men.

I got on well with Charlton. At every bait time he would give me an apple or an orange, and on a Friday he would give me a shilling. This was his way of thanking me for helping him to fill some of his tubs and for carrying his tin of explosives.

He was 74 when he was forced into compulsory retirement. He died a few months later.

Bill Rothery was the colliery overman, or master shifter, at Prestwick. I have worked at three different collieries and known most of the officials, but Bill Rothery stands out head and shoulders above them all. He was small in stature but had the heart of a lion. I have seen men cringe with fear at the sound of his voice or in the knowledge that he was about to come and visit them. He was extremely bad tempered and impatient, but he was very fair and he would never ask anyone to do something he couldn't do himself. At times he was a jolly man with a good sense of humour, but whenever trouble arose you had to watch out, he could swear non-stop for about a minute and never use the same swear word twice!

His office on the surface was between the explosives shed and the winding engine house, and most of the workmen would pass it on the way to the baths. He would peer out of his window and make a mental note of every man as they went by. On one occasion he'd noticed that one man had just turned up for work after being off the previous day. He shouted out to the man, 'Where the bloody hell were ye yesterday?' The worker replied, 'I'm sorry Bill, but I buried the wife's brother yesterday.' 'Bloody hell man. Can you not get the useless buggers to die in the middle of the week and bury them at the weekend!' He didn't mean it, it was just his sense of humour.

On, another occasion, my cousin Matty, who operated the cutting machine, had encountered some difficulty in cutting the coalface due to pressure on the cutting jib. It was a common problem but meant a delay in the cutting operation. Normally it took about an hour to correct, but on this occasion it had taken several hours to put right. This meant delaying the start of the filling shift. So incensed was Bill Rothery on hearing the length of the delay that he exclaimed, 'How can it be humanly possible for a man to circle the globe three times in the length of time it takes Matty Graham to free a bloody useless fast jib.' He was referring to Yuri Gagarin, the Russian astronaut who was the first man in space to circle the earth.

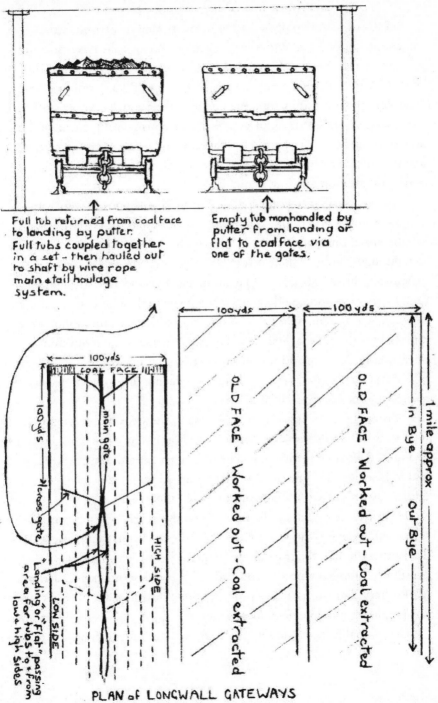

Full tub returned from coal face to landing by putter. Full tubs coupled together in a set - then hauled out to shaft by wire rope main & tail houlage system.

Empty tub manhandled by putter from landing or flat to coal face via one of the gates.

PLAN of LONGWALL GATEWAYS

Bill Rothery was so dedicated to his work that he arrived at the colliery at 12 noon and didn't leave until one o'clock the next morning. He worked a 12-hour shift every day and sometimes more. He would even come to the pit on a Sunday morning from 9.30am until noon to make sure that everything was prepared for the Sunday evening shift.

He didn't smoke, drink or gamble, most unusual for a bachelor. His only pleasure in life appeared to be his car, and going to the pictures on a Saturday afternoon, although, occasionally, he would have a couple of bottles of stout on a Saturday night.

The system of extracting coal at Prestwick was known as longwall gateways, and was very old fashioned. The longwall, or coalface, was usually about one hundred yards long, with a series of roadways running at right angles away from it. Every 100 yards that the face advanced, meant that the flat also had to be advanced. This involved lifting the double tracks, advancing them and then relaying them, and extending the rope haulage system. When the double tracks had been lifted they were replaced by a set of single tracks. This was the major underground operation at the time and was always carried out under the watchful eye of Bill Rothery. So critical was the job of relaying the points that he trusted no one but himself to do it.

This operation was always carried out at the weekend. It usually took four shifts to complete. It was started on Friday evening and would be finished by Sunday morning. The haulage rope and return wheel also had to be extended. The siting of the return wheel anchor stay was critical, again this was carried out only by Bill Rothery.

He asked me to work a double shift on the Friday. My job was to salvage all the nails and wood sleepers as the track was being lifted. As Bill Rothery re-laid the track, I was responsible for keeping him constantly supplied with the salvaged nails. It was so amusing watching Mr Rothery that I would have probably done the job without receiving any pay, never mind being paid overtime.

Occasionally, he would hit his finger or thumb while knocking in a

LONGWALL GATEWAY SYSTEM - CROSS SECTION

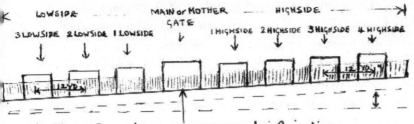

LOWSIDE   MAIN or MOTHER GATE   HIGHSIDE

3 LOWSIDE   2 LOWSIDE   1 LOWSIDE   1 HIGHSIDE   2 HIGHSIDE   3 HIGHSIDE   4 HIGHSIDE

12 YDS

Incline of coal seam approx 1 in 8 incline

CROSS-SECTION of LONGWALL GATEWAYS APPROX 100 YDS

'Gate' is mining term for tunnel or roadway

Eight gates supplying tubs to the coal face

Each gate is approx 12 yards centre-centre.

So each coal filler has 12 yards of coal face to fill into tubs

Therefore 8 gates × 12 yds = 96 yds + 2 yds each end of face
gives a total of 100 yds (approx)

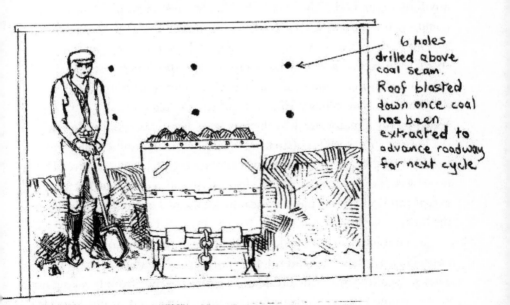

6 holes drilled above coal seam. Roof blasted down once coal has been extracted to advance roadway for next cycle

COAL FILLER FILLING TUB AT MAIN GATE

nail and then he would start to swear and curse. At the same time, he would look along the tunnel and if he caught sight of anyone dodging work or taking a rest they would get the full blast of his temper. The tone of his voice would change from a loud bellow to a hoarse whisper as he tried to get all his words out in one breath. Then suddenly his mood would change into a complete calm. He would give out a giggle, and then winking at me he would say 'There, that's wakened the buggers up!'

Despite his bad temper and swearing, he was respected by all the workmen, officials and management. His feeling of responsibility towards the pit was above and beyond the call of duty. Several times I have seen him put the pit before his own safety.

He would never leave the colliery at the end of the shift unless everything was ready for coal production to begin in the next shift. It was his personal dedication that rubbed off on to some of the officials and workmen. His motto was that the pit should always come before anything or anybody. The pit was his life, his second home. In fact, you could say that he was married to it.

Bill Rothery was probably the biggest influence on me. The thing that I admired the most was his complete confidence in himself. I have seen him working alone on a coalface when conditions were so dangerous that no other workmen or official would go near. Occasionally a major break at the face would cause the roof to lower, the floor to lift, the sides of roadways could crumble, timber supports would crack like carrots and the whole place seemed to come alive. The noise was deafening and it put the fear of God into everyone, everyone except Bill Rothery. He had an uncanny knack of knowing exactly when the break was about to occur.

When it happened, I would have to supply him with wood chock nobs. He used these to build solid supports from the floor to the roof. They helped to control the break and prevent the roof from breaking off at the coalface. They also kept the face tunnel open and stopped the face

LONGWALL GATEWAY SYSTEM - PLAN

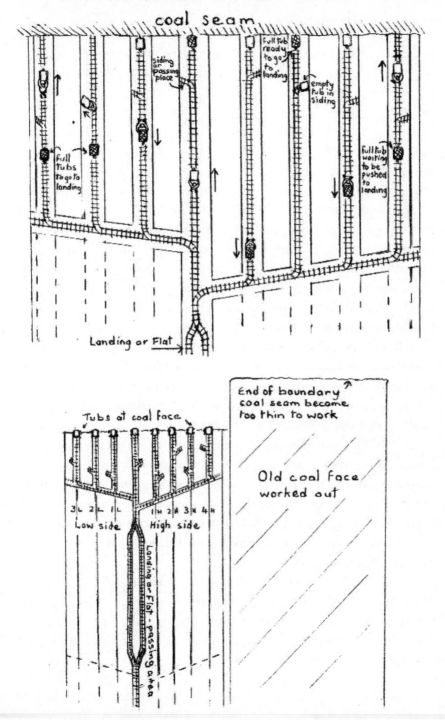

coal seam

siding or passing place

full tub ready to go to landing

empty tub in siding

full tubs to go to landing

full tub waiting to be pushed to landing

Landing or Flat

Tubs at coal face

End of boundary coal seam became too thin to work

Old coal face worked out

3 L   2 L   1 L   1 H   2 H   3 H   4 H
Low side   High side

Landing or Flat - passing area

from being lost and having to be won out again. All the time he would be cursing and swearing at the workmen for being cowards and not helping him to save the face. After a while the noise would stop, the dust would settle and the wood supports stopped snapping. Calm would return.

After a break, Bill Rothery would inspect the coalface to assess what damage had been done, taking note of the work needed to allow the cutting machine to traverse the face once again. Although still only 17, and not yet face trained, I was curious to see for myself what conditions on the face were like after a major break. The roof had lowered all along the face and a large crack that was between 12 and 15 inches wide had formed in the roof. Not only had the roof lowered, it had also moved away from the face. The crack here was so large that with a naked flame it was impossible to see how far it went. It was so enormous that you could have easily crawled into the crevice as the angle of the break was forty five degrees to the face.

Bill Rothery and some other workmen actually did crawl into the crevice to insert short wood props to support the roof. It was mining at its most skilful, where experience was essential but it was unbelievably dangerous. You had to be constantly aware of the stones, which might suddenly dislodge themselves and come tumbling down on top of you.

In 1955 Prestwick was still a naked flame pit. The danger from a methane gas explosion was said to be non existent, but rumours had started to circulate that methane gas had been found in the developments of the Brockwell seam. One of the development workers was pushing an empty tub into the workings when he found to his amazement that the flame from his carbide lamp ignited the methane gas that was present and actually caused a miniature explosion.

A few months later I was cavilled to the development's 'arc walls', where this had occurred, and I worked with the man concerned. Tom E., known by his mates as 'chicken', described what had happened. 'Everything just went up in a blue flash, and things got kinda warm,' he said with a sarcastic grin. Most of the hairs on his body were singed or burnt as all he was wearing was a pair of trousers and a vest. Apparently it was all over in seconds and he was found several minutes later by his putter, lying prostrate on the ground. His injuries weren't as severe as they might have been and he was back at work the following week. The incident was all hushed up, and soon forgotten about.

My first experience with methane gas happened when I was only 17. Bill Rothery came to the district where I was working; it was a new face, just recently won out, and I was only a spare, not yet cavilled to production. 'Come with me young un,' he said, and I followed him to the first working place above the main roadway, No.1 highside. 'I'll show you how to get rid of bloody spunky gas,' he mumbled.

At that time he always carried a hand-held carbide lamp with an enormous round, shiny, brass reflector. He lifted his lamp to the roof and nothing happened. The large reflector prevented the flame from reaching the ceilings. 'Give me your lamp,' he said. Taking my lamp from my cloth cap I handed it to him; it was a third of the size of his lamp with a much smaller reflector. He crawled several feet further up the face and lifted the naked flame to the roof. WHOOSH! The whole face was suddenly lit up by tongues of blue flame that rippled away into the distance. It was like being in the bowels of hell. For a few moments the whole face was lit up by flames and then thrown into complete darkness. Our own lamps had also been blown out in the sudden draught.

I was only a few feet away from Bill Rothery and I could hear him cursing my lamp as he tried to relight it. 'Bloody hell, what was that?' I asked him. 'That's how to get rid of bloody spunky gas,' he replied. On relighting my lamp he again lifted it to the roof. WHOOSH! The same thing happened, only this time it was much slower. The flames licked their way up the face before suddenly disappearing.

This time our lamps didn't go out and Bill Rothery tried once more to burn off the gas. However, this time nothing happened. We crawled further up the face, trying again at different intervals but all the gas had been burned off. We had been in the middle of the face when the gas had ignited and I estimated that the flames must have been about 50 yards long. There was no one working on the return side which is just as well, otherwise they would have been severely burned.

This method of burning off gas was used in pre-Victorian times and was the cause of most major mining disasters. It was illegal in a naked flame pit, but who could tell the difference between a deliberate act and an accident? Bill Rothery told me to tell no one about what I had just witnessed and I kept my promise.

On reflection, and after having been educated about the dangers of methane gas, I shudder to think what might have happened. If the percentage of methane gas present in the air had exceeded five per cent, I would not have been here to write this book. And how was Bill Rothery to know what percentage there was?

When he had been igniting the gas, two men were working at the lower end of the face, preparing it to be cut. As there was no method of dust suppression at the time, once the cutting operation had got under way the whole air stream would have been filled with very fine coal dust, providing the perfect ingredients for a major explosion. Had Bill Rothery arrived at the district a few minutes later or had the cutting operation commenced a few minutes earlier, only God knows what would have happened.

Shortly after my experience with methane, I heard that the overman in the fore-shift, a Mr Scott, had burnt off some gas in a coal filling operation and proudly went to report it to the colliery manager. I'm told that the manager hit the roof – he was furious and could not believe the man's stupidity. Mr Scott had only a few weeks to go before retirement but was forced to leave a little sooner than he intended!

On another occasion, I was putting tubs to a filler called Tommy F. He was working a section just below my cousin, John George (Uncle Ernie's son). John George was a massive bloke, six feet tall and weighing about 16 stone, but he was as gentle as a lamb. 'Come here,' said

Tommy, 'and watch this.' I crawled onto the face from the tunnel and I could see John George throwing coals towards his roadway.

Tommy took off his cloth cap and lit up a cigarette. He then lifted his lamp to a small break in the roof. WHOOSH! Tongues of flames licked their way up the face just a few inches from the roof and past John George. He got such a shock, and shouted down to Tommy 'Pack it in, you bloody idiot. I nearly got burnt.' Tommy pretended not to hear him and shouted up the face 'What was that, bonny lad?' 'Stop messing about!' he yelled. 'Sorry bonny lad,' said Tommy grinning from ear to ear, 'me lamp must have touched the breaker!'

God! Here was a situation where men were actually playing about with methane gas underground, ignorant of its incredible danger. There appeared to be some blind loyalty to the pit, no one ever reported the presence of the gas. They felt that if the mining inspectorate found out about it, they might close the pit.

Eventually, senior management did get to know of the presence of gas; their response was comical. The coal fillers and putters working on the highside of the face were issued with electric cap lamps and smoking here was prohibited. Men working on the lowside continued to use naked lights!

The manager's deputy, who was in charge of the district, issued instructions to all workmen that they were not allowed to smoke because of the gassy conditions, but little or no notice was taken. Eventually all workmen in the Brockwell seam were issued with safety cap lamps and smoking was prohibited throughout the district.

We had a situation where half the pit was using safety lamps while those in the Busty seam still worked with naked flames. However, several weeks later the whole pit became a safety lamp pit and no one was allowed to smoke. But some men, having been used to smoking underground all of their working lives took badly to it and continued to ignore the ban. Some went to great lengths to smuggle cigarettes and matches underground; they would hide them in their bait tins, behind their caps, or even sew special pockets in their shorts. One man went as far as to hide them in a knotted condom inside his thermos flask!

All of this eventually stopped after an incident involving poor Herby. One morning, after a spot check at the bottom of the shaft, Herby was found to have five cigarettes and a box of matches in his possession. He was fined £5 and given a week's notice. However, he was later reinstated after much pleading by the NUM. But the incident served as a strong warning to anyone thinking of continuing the habit underground and smoking stopped completely.

It was while I was working as a hand putter that face training was introduced at Prestwick. Previously, putters had had to go to North Walbottle to receive their training. At first men were only trained for two operations – filling and stonework (preparing, making and advancing roadways). But when conveyors were introduced to the face, men were instructed on how to advance these as well.

Operating the coal cutting machine was thought to be too difficult and too dangerous for the ordinary workman and only men specially selected by senior management were given this training. Selection for face training was taken from the cavilling list of putters in order of seniority. As I was only 17, and a long way down the list, I thought I would never become face-trained.

Owing to the new roadway and haulage system, production was steadily increasing week by week and 400 tubs of coal a shift became a reality. The coal seam increased in thickness by a few inches and I can remember quite vividly the first time 400 tubs of coal were produced in one shift.

The overman during day shift, was like a cat on a hot tin roof. We had achieved 397 tubs in the previous shift and he knew that the magical 400 figure was about to be reached. I was putting for my brother Reg that day. It was nearing the end of the shift as I came from the face to the flat with the 398th tub. The overman looked ill with worry. 'Has Reg got any coal left?' he inquired. 'I think so,' I said. 'Well hurry up, hurry up,' he said, anxiously taking out his pocket watch from his waistcoat to check the time.

When I got to the face, Reg was just topping off the last tub. I thought we had failed again to reach the magic figure of 400. On returning to the 'flat' I found the overman literally dancing up and down with joy, my tub was the 401st. As I approached him he ran alongside me and clapped me on the back, I've never seen a man who was so happy and excited. The overman had to sit down – the excitement was almost too much for him. He took off his shiny black helmet and wiped the sweat off his head; he was as bald as Yul Brynner.

A few minutes later he phoned the under-manager's office to tell him the good news but neither the manager or the under-manager was in; they were both at a meeting with the area manager. When the overman arrived at the surface, the under-manager was still not in his office. The manager's clerk, told me of the pained looked of disappointment on the overman's face at not being able to tell him the good news first hand.

The whole pit seemed to be buzzing with excitement. I even heard Mam and Aunty Ginny talking about it at the back gate as Aunty Ginny was cleaning Uncle Mat's pit clothes. It was a marvellous feeling to be part of the record-breaking shift, I really felt somebody and very, very proud as I was beginning to live up to the good name of the Grahams. Later on, every time I came into contact with the overman I could do nothing wrong. As he had no children of his own, I felt almost like his adopted son.

When I was still at school I used to dig his garden for him: he had trouble with his back and hated gardening. I was rewarded for this by being able to watch the first televised FA Cup Final from Wembley. The overman was the first and only man to own a television in the terrace at that time.

The overman was very likeable but often did stupid things without thinking. One day he was re-socketing a steel rope that had become damaged and frayed. He cut off the damaged piece of rope and proceeded to re-socket that instead of the good rope. He did this in front of an audience of men who were having their bait while waiting for the rope to be repaired. They realised what he had done but said nothing. When he had finished the men started to cheer and give him a standing ovation. Filled with rage and temper after realising his stupidity, he threw his tools down the roadway, only to realise that he still needed them. This inflamed his temper even more, much to the delight of the workers. Eventually he calmed down and saw the funny side of it.

I heard one story about him receiving a clock from a relative in Canada. According to the overman there wasn't another clock like it in the world. However, after a while the clock stopped and it refused to start again. The only way it would work was in a backward tilting position so the overman sawed half an inch off both back legs of the sideboard!

As the months went by I became an accomplished putter and I could supply the best fillers with as many tubs as they required. I could also negotiate the most arduous roadways as well, if not better, than any other man.

The amount of coal being filled by hand was phenomenal. My brother Reg held the weekly tonnage record of 141 tons, 15 cwts. The daily record of tubs filled was somewhere in the eighties. Every filler who produced over 100 tons in a week was given ten shillings from the manager's own pocket as a bonus. It was quite common for putters to help the fillers fill the tubs towards the end of a shift, even though it was illegal if they had not been face-trained. The older men like Uncle Ernie and Charlton relied on this help; the younger men like Reg didn't, simply because it took a putter all his time to keen him supplied.

It was while doing this illegal filling that an untrained filler received an injury from a roof fall. The putter should not have been on the face and he received a heavy warning from the Deputy. After that incident, the help stopped.

Putters' rates of pay were determined by the distance they had to travel from the flat to the face. A standard rate of £1 was paid for the first 80 yards, increasing by a shilling for every extra ten yards. In rough terms it worked out to be just over a shilling per tub. As a putter could enhance the filler's total by as many as ten tubs by helping him to fill, not helping him cost the putter, on average, ten shilling a day or £2.10s a week. It's easy to imagine the feelings of the putters when they were no longer allowed to help the fillers!

A new face had been made ready for production and it was the beginning of a new quarter. I was cavilled first out of the hat and so I had first claim on the new district. I decided that I would try and supply two men with tubs instead of one! That way I wouldn't waste time waiting for tubs to be filled, I would be supplying more tubs and would earn more money.

Billy H., the most senior putter at the time, told me that I was mad even to attempt such a gruelling task. 'Slavery was abolished over 100 years ago,' he said, 'and you're trying to bring it back. Anyway, you'll never manage it.' When someone tells me something can't be done, it makes me all the more determined to do it.

Being cavilled on the lowside workings, I at least had the assistance of a small electric winch that hauled the full tubs up the cross-gate roadway. So instead of pushing one tub at a time, I decided to push two. Once my system was established I began achieving mind-boggling results. It had been known for a putter to supply eighty tubs in a shift, but now I was supplying over 90. I soon reached the magic figure of 100 tubs in a single shift for a whole week. These figures were previously unheard of, but I did it. And it wasn't just a flash in the pan either, I went on to achieve results like this for the next six months.

I was probably one of the highest paid miners in Northumberland, if not the highest. My earnings averaged between £26 and £27 a week, almost double the county average and I was only 18 years old. The work was extremely strenuous, but not as demanding as it was to work the highside, thanks to the assistance of the electric winch. Putting 25 score tubs in a week was probably a national record but because the method of extracting coal at Prestwick was about to change and a new era of mining was dawning, not much notice was taken of these fantastic results, or so I thought.

3 Accidents and experiences

My turn came to be cavilled for coalface training, but, as I was only 18 years old, the safety and training officer, thought that I was still too young and so again I missed my turn on the list. I was so disappointed that I thought of chucking it in altogether and applying to join the Royal Navy. It didn't seem fair at all.

I'm not sure what happened next but someone must have relented. Whether it was the manager, or safety and training officer I'm not sure, but anyway I got to do my training. Training took 16 weeks – eight weeks on the coal filling operation and eight weeks on stonework. Part of the coalface had been designated for the training operation and my Uncle Mat and Charlton were the two filling supervisors. I was assigned to Uncle Mat for the next eight weeks, and placed under his personal supervision at the coalface.

Training consisted of learning how to lay track, drill, hew and fill undercut coals into tubs and set supports according to the manager's rules. While I was being trained I was paid the average of my previous month's wages which was £25 per week.

The colliery manager, decided that a new method of extracting coal was necessary because of a change in the gradient of the seam. This change signalled the beginning of the end of an era. Hand filling and hand putting would cease, ending one of the cruellest jobs ever invented.

Before the new system could begin, one more face had to be worked under the old system. And it was on this last face that I did my coal filling training. It took quite a while to get used to filling tubs on my knees for the whole shift. About half of the coal could be filled straight into the tubs but the rest of the coals had to be shovelled twice, into the roadway and then into the tub. The seam was three feet high, perfect for filling. Later on I had the experience of filling from a two feet seam, this was torture. Imagine kneeling with your back against the roof, your chin almost touching the floor and then trying to shovel coal!

Knowing where, when and how to set supports was where you had to rely on the skill and experience of the supervisor; if you didn't it made the job much more difficult. Once you had extracted coal it exposed more roof which obviously had to be supported. By tapping the roof gently with an axe or hewing pick you could determine whether it was broken or fractured by the noise it gave off. This was known as 'jowelling the roof'.

Filling coals was physically demanding but very boring. It took about 40 shovels to fill one tub. To alleviate the boredom, I used to treat work as exercise, rocking back and forward it would be in, out, up and over, in, out, up and over, again and again. A trainee and his supervisor would fill an average of around 15 to 20 tons of coal per shift depending on the supply of empties. Priority was always given to the trained fillers over the trainees whenever there was a delay in supply.

I did my stonework training on a new face under the new system. No one at the colliery had had any previous experience of this way of working but the manager wanted the best workmen cavilled to this face as the future of the colliery depended on it. After several union debates, the NUM gave its blessings and the manager got his wish.

The work was still physically demanding. The main difference was that the number of roadways leading to the face was reduced from nine to three. Instead of the coal being hand putted to the 'flat', it was moved via a conveyor belt and placed into a set of tubs at the 'flat' before being taken to the shaft using the original haulage system.

The face now had two tracks running along its entire length. One allowed the cutting machine to traverse back and forth, undercutting the seam, the other housed the conveyor. This method was already out of date when it reached Prestwick, nevertheless it was a big improvement.

Coal was conveyed along the face tunnel in a large steel box (skip), one end of which was open while the other had a hinged flap that scraped the coals along. This track had spill boards on either side of it which acted as a guide for the skip. It was powered by an electric winch in the tail-gate roadway. Two skips were attached to a steel rope so one could be at the loading gate (in the centre of the face and at right angles to it) while the other was at the end of the face. One skip pushed and scraped the coals from the left side of the face and the other did it from the right. It was very crude but effective and quickly produced good results.

The first really serious accident I encountered underground occurred when I was doing my face training. It was almost the end of the shift and I was following the last tub out from the lowside workings. There were four full tubs being hauled up the incline towards the main roadway. The putter in charge of them was Jimmy B. Being a tall lad, Jimmy found it easier to get up the incline by grasping the handle of the last tub with both hands and being helped up by the motion of the winch. The roadway was just over tub height, three-and-a-half feet, and the same in width. The incline was one in eight.

The four tubs, coupled together in a train, were about to negotiate the turn onto the main roadway when, for some unknown reason, the first tub became uncoupled from the steel haulage rope. All four tubs began running back down the incline. Realising what was happening, but with very little space in which to do anything, Jimmy stepped to the side of the roadway. He had his back to the tunnel but because he was so tall his chest and head were curved under the roof. Pressing as hard as he could with his back to the wall and roof, he tried to allow the train to run past him. But as the train was now free from its haulage rope it was very quickly gathering speed and the coals protruding from the top of the tub caught his chest and carried him down the incline, turning him over and over, crushing him between the roof top and the coal tub.

Before the accident it was as if I'd had a premonition of what was about to happen. Normally, I would have followed right behind the train, up the incline. But on this occasion, I waited at the first roadway for the tubs to be hauled up the incline and around the turn onto the main roadway. When I saw the tubs running back along the roadway I dived into an old working, opposite the turn of the first lowside roadway. This caused my lamp to go out and I was now in complete darkness.

I heard the tubs go rushing past and Jimmy screaming with pain as he was dragged between the roof and the coal tub. There was a huge crash and then silence. Eventually I relit my lamp and managed to crawl up to where the tubs had become derailed. Coal had been spilled all around, the first tub was lying on its side almost empty, the second and third tubs were jack-knifed against the roof, Jimmy was squashed on top of the fourth tub. He was lying on his back in a crab-like position and screaming with agony.

By the time I got to him, more workers had arrived on the scene. 'Get the Deputy,' I shouted. 'He's on his way,' someone replied. 'Where's the stretcher? We'll need the stretcher,' I screamed.

Freeing Jimmy is something I'll never forget. He was wedged between the top of the tub and the roof. Every attempt we made to force him free, he cried out in pain. We eventually freed him, by which time the Deputy had arrived. He gave him first aid and we placed him on a stretcher and carried him almost two miles to the shaft. That journey to the shaft seemed endless.

Jimmy never worked underground again. He suffered from a fractured pelvis, broken and crushed ribs, and a right hand that was now useless. He did, however, return to work at the pit. He was given a light job on the surface, cleaning out tubs.

A later investigation found that the pin attaching the rope couplings to the links of the first tub had worked loose, this coincided with an uneven build-up of rope on the winching drum, causing the rope to whiplash, which then led the rope to uncouple itself. A stay on the last tub failed to operate and prevent the runaway. Runaways were common in those days, but as long as no one was seriously hurt, no action was taken. However, after this accident a new type of anchor-stay was introduced and anyone found not using it would be fined and threatened with their notice.

Because speed was essential when putting, putters seldom used the stays and the officials usually turned a blind eye. Of course it was wrong not to use the safety device, but it was common practice.

Making and preparing roadways underground was referred to by a different name at different pits. You could be known as a caunchman, a ripper or tunneller. At Prestwick, you were a stoneman. Stonework training entailed drilling and boring holes into the rock face immediately above the coalface. This space was known as the 'caunch' or 'ripping lip'. You usually had to bore between six and ten holes, depending on the size of the roadway you were tunnelling.

The boring was done with an electric rotary drilling machine. Sometimes as many as four men were needed to push against the machine, depending on the hardness of the rock. Often the machine would get so hot that it became impossible to touch and you had to stop boring for some time to allow it to cool down.

Makeshift platforms were put up to enable you to reach the upper part of the 'ripping-lip'. But it was common practice to bore for the next preparation immediately after shot firing had been completed, using a mountain of stones as your next platform.

The majority of men were loath to pick up the drilling machine as it took a good deal of strength to operate. If you were drilling through tiny fractures in the rock, the machine would stop and if you were not careful It could give you a nasty blow as it whipped out of your hands. This had been known to break wrists and knock men unconscious.

A worker had been killed while drilling the coalface at a neighbouring colliery. After having his bait he returned to the face with only a few more holes to go and decided to leave his scarf around his neck. It became tangled in the drilling rod and he choked to death.

After drilling was completed the holes were charged with explosives, stemmed with clay and then fired. Around 20 tons of stone would come tumbling to the floor, leaving an empty cavity above. This cavity formed the advancing roadway. It had to be secured and supported using two steel arched girders. The stones were thrown into the tunnel that had been created when the coal was extracted and stowed from the floor to the roof on each side of the roadway. This was known as the 'pack' and actually helped to support the roadway. Constant pressure from the strata above eventually caused the pack to form a solid structure.

Some workmen were so skilled at building packs that it looked like random stonework and some people thought it was a beauty to behold. All the stones had to be stored in this fashion, none were transported to the surface – stones didn't pay the wages.

There were three men employed on the new roadway as well as myself and another trainee. Our job was to transfer the stones from where they had been blasted, by throwing them down the tunnel to the workmen who built the pack. The face travelled in a southerly direction, dipping steeply. Eventually water started dripping from the roof, slowly at first, but gradually increasing. The conditions were so bad that all men in the district were provided with oilskins. Working underground in oilskins is one of the most unpleasant experiences I have ever had.

I would be working at such speed, shovelling and throwing stones for at least two thirds of the shift, that when I came to take off the oilskins I was literally dripping wet and my underclothes were saturated. I found it easier to discard my oilskins and work with as little clothing on as possible, leaving me with dry clothes to put back on at the end of the shift.

Roof conditions at the face quickly deteriorated. With water seeping through the roof the strata immediately above the seam became friable and difficult to support. Extra supports had to be used to overcome this problem. However, perseverance prevailed and eventually conditions improved and water stopped dripping through.

FILLING and PUTTING OPERATION at COAL FACE

View from side

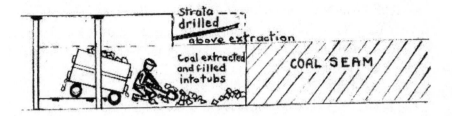

Strata drilled above extraction

Coal extracted and filled into tubs

COAL SEAM

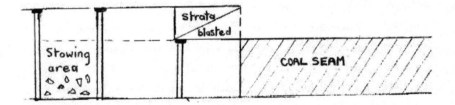

Strata blasted

Stowing area

COAL SEAM

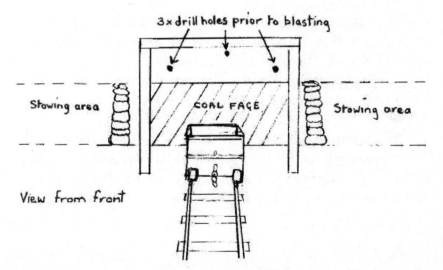

3 x drill holes prior to blasting

Stowing area

COAL FACE

Stowing area

View from front

When I finished my training I was sent back to the district where I had previously worked. During this period I was a spare filler and covered for absentees. Some days I would have to fill coal and supply my own tubs. Imagine having to fill a tub of coal at the face, push it along a narrow roadway for anything between 100 and 120 yards to the 'flat', and then return with an empty tub, only to repeat the whole process over and over again. The physical effort involved was stupendous. On one occasion I actually managed to supply myself with and fill 44 tubs. That was a few more than many fillers could manage with the help of a putter.

I often think back and wonder why it was we worked so hard, especially in conditions that were, at times, inhumane. Almost everyone had a blind loyalty to the pit, and success did give you a strong sense of self-respect. Everyone worked hard for themselves and if you got an extra pound it was because you'd earned it. Everyone knew everyone else, and everyone seemed to be happy doing what they were doing.

Once a fortnight, on a Friday morning at the end of a fore-shift, all my mates would gather at 'me Mam's' for a cup of tea. We would discuss the events of the previous week as well as the pit's future. At the time, there was much excitement because rumour had it that conveyors were about to be introduced on the face and roadways at Prestwick. A new age was dawning for us lads.

The present 'skip' face at the pit was now well established and producing excellent results. But even at its inception it was out of date and old fashioned. One of its disadvantages was that it often caused roof falls; as the steel boxes traversed the face they would sometimes draw out the roof supports. These falls had to be cleared before production could continue.

The signalling operation controlling the movement of the skip was very elementary. It consisted of a thin wire which stretched the length of the face. Pulling on this wire operated an electric bell. The winch operator would interpret these signals to stop or start the 'skip', and

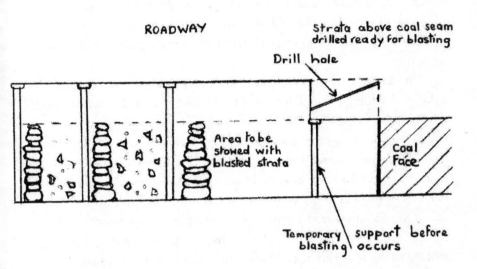

ROADWAY

Strata above coal seam drilled ready for blasting

Drill hole

Area to be stowed with blasted strata

Coal Face

Temporary support before blasting occurs

control its direction.

Production reached a staggering figure, over 200 tons a day, and 1,100 tons in a week. And this was probably the most productive face of its kind in the county.

Every Friday, after they had collected their pay, my two brothers, Cyril and Reg, would call in to see Mam. If they didn't, they got a good ticking off and were asked to explain why they hadn't visited. Mam liked to keep everyone in the family in touch, and like a mother hen, she still looked after her brood.

It was on one of these visits that our Cyril told me that the manager wanted to see me. 'What on earth for?' I said. 'I don't know,' said Cyril, 'But you better get over there double quick.' 'Put on your good suit and smarten yourself up,' said Mam, and this I did – or was made to do!

It took only a couple of minutes to reach his office. As I approached,

I wondered what it was I had done wrong. The clerk's door was always open and so I marched in. 'Hello John,' said the manager's clerk, whose father was one of the winding operators. 'What can I do for you?' 'I've got an appointment,' 'I said nervously. 'Just a minute,' he said, and disappeared next door. I could feel myself getting more and more nervous but I tried not to show it. Jack came back out, 'You can go in,' he said.

The manager was sitting behind his highly polished wooden desk, his bald head shining through his silver hair, which matched a well-trimmed 'Hitler style' moustache. I stood nervously in front of his desk. 'How would you like to operate the coal-cutting machine?' he grumbled. I just stood there speechless. 'Well, how about it?' I could detect a gleam in his eyes. 'A've never had anything to do with the coal-cutters,' I replied. 'I know that. But I'm prepared to have you trained,' he said, 'when I can afford to put someone in your place. I was let down last Sunday and I can't afford to have my key workers letting me down. Anyway, he's retiring in the near future and I want to have you trained to take his place.' 'Thank you very much,' I stammered and left his office.

I walked home as if in a vale of clouds, I just couldn't believe it. At only 19 years old I was being offered one of the key jobs at the pit. Cyril was still talking to Mam when I got home and they both asked why he'd wanted to see me. 'He wants me to go on the cutters,' I exclaimed proudly. I saw the look of disappointment fall across Mam's face: she knew only too well that operating the cutting-machine was one of the most dangerous jobs in mining. It was quite common in small mining villages for cutter-men to be seriously injured or even killed.

Mam turned to Cyril. 'He's too young to learn the cutters!' she exclaimed. 'Don't worry,' said Cyril. 'He'll get the best training available, and he'll probably be sent with our Matty.' Matty was noted for being the best cutter operator at the colliery. 'He won't be allowed to touch the machine for a long time. He'll just be allowed to watch and take notice of what's happening.' This seemed to pacify her, but she was obviously still very sceptical.

While I was waiting to be trained for the coal-cutting machine a four-man team was required for the development of the Busty seam. The team consisted of a putter, a filler, a stoneman, and a cutter operator. It was known as composite work and was a continuous form of mining; as soon as each operation was completed the next one began. The job entailed driving a roadway through 200 yards of solid rock and coal. Gordon T. was the filler, Bob Y. the stoneman, Nickel F. the cutting machine operator and I was the putter.

On a normal production face it took 24 hours to complete a cycle and by the end of the week, five cycles had been completed. For example, boring and cutting were done in one shift, filling and putting in another shift, and the roadway would be made in the third shift, thus completing a cycle. But by beginning each operation as soon as the previous one was complete, regardless of whether or not a shift had ended, we were completing six or seven cycles in a week.

Driving the roadway had almost been completed when I was sent to do my coal cutting training. This was in the Brockwell seam and the supervisor was to be my cousin Matty. At first I was just a dogsbody doing menial tasks and not being allowed near the cutting machine. I was taught how to make and prepare the tunnel for the machine to travel in. This could be quite dangerous as face supports had to be removed to accommodate the machine, causing the roof to 'weight on' and induce a roof break at the face. A 550 volt electric cable, 150 yards long had to be dragged onto the face by hand to supply the machine with power.

The cutter was used in the preparation of the coalface before production began. It cut out the bottom section of the seam. Explosives were inserted into the face of the seam and fired. The explosion caused the face to fragment and shatter onto the undercut. If the face was not undercut first, the explosives would merely create a bigger hole instead of shattering the whole face.

After the machine had undercut the coalface, it had to be turned 180 degrees before it could cut the face in the opposite direction. The jib remained in position but the body of the machine would be swivelled round. This was the most dangerous aspect of the operation and it had to be done at both ends of the face. After mastering this technique, the rest would be relatively simple.

The pick settings and lines, that is, their distance apart and the length of the pick protruding from the cutting chain, was a closely guarded secret and individual cuttermen were loath to share their experience. Each cutterman used his own gauge to determine the pick setting – this was most important as it eventually determined the line of the next cut. If the picks were not set correctly the jib would not run parallel with the seam but would either cut into the floor or would be cutting the seam at an angle and thus not tunnelling out all of the coal.

The cutter tried to cut the floor of the seam without leaving any coal underneath the cutting jib. If, for example, three inches of coal were left under the jib, it meant that the seam would be three inches shorter and some production would be lost. And it could be the difference between heaven and hell in terms of working conditions, especially in thin seams where, believe me, an extra three inches of height made the world of difference.

Cuttermen worked in pairs. There were two pairs of cutters at Prestwick, one in the Brockwell seam and one in the Busty seam. My cousin Matty and Gabe G. worked in the Brockwell seam, and George and Robert (Matty's brothers) worked in the Busty seam. One man operated the machine while the other followed behind, resetting supports and inserting nogs of wood in the under coal to prevent the bore holes collapsing. The nogs also acted as temporary supports until the face had been fired.

The starting times of their shifts were determined, as they were at most collieries, by the fillers, who were the 'glory boys'. At Prestwick cuttermen worked afternoon and night-shift, alternating weekly. This meant that you had no social life during the week, unless you got an early finish on the afternoon shift which meant that you could have two or three pints in the local before 10.30 pm.

The machine had no means of dust suppression. The only protection available was dust masks which you placed over your nose and mouth. Every other day the machine would cut coal in the direction opposite to the air current. This meant that the dust was carried away by the airstream and conditions weren't quite so bad. But when it cut in the other direction, dust conditions were atrocious. The cutting machine was the largest piece of face machinery we used. It was nine feet long, two feet wide and 15 inches high, with a jib that worked just like a circular saw, extending four-and-a-half feet into the floor of the seam when in the cutting position. The jib, with its rotating picks, was pulled along the floor of the seam until it had cut into an angle of 90 degrees. It then locked in that position and sawed its way along the face. The cutting machine was attached to a steel wire rope, 90 feet long with a small loop at the end which allowed it to be anchored to a stay hammered between the floor and the roof at an angle of 45 degrees. The machine hauled and scraped its way along the coal seam pulling itself towards the anchor.

This is where the skill of the operator became apparent. If the cutting picks were set correctly, the cutting horizon could be controlled and every inch of coal would be hollowed out. If not, you would either cut into the stone floor, or leave behind a coal floor which should not be there. A good cutter was worth his weight in gold, as it was this man who would either make or break the face.

The operator worked from a position immediately in front of the machine crawling slowly backwards, checking all the while that the natural seam was being followed. You had to keep an eye on the colour of the small coals which were being churned out from the face. If they were black you should be doing all right, if they turned slightly grey it meant that you were starting to cut through stone.

Dust created by cutting coal was nothing compared to the dust created when cutting through stone. This occurred if the cutter was not properly aligned to the natural seam, or if he was cutting through a fault. Cutting through a stone fault meant you couldn't see a hand in front of you for dust and the machine had to be slowed down as much as possible. Periodically you had to stop the machine to allow the dust to settle so that you could see what you were doing. At times the stone was so hard, the picks became blunt and blunt picks created even more dust. When this happened the machine had to be stopped so that the picks could be changed.

The heat given off from the engine of the cutter was, at times, unbearable, especially in such a confined space. And the noise it created was horrendous, piercing your forehead. All of this, added to the dust, meant that you had a constant headache, but you just had to accept this and get on with your job.

When the machine reached the anchor stay, the anchor would be removed and transferred 90 feet up the face. This would be repeated until the whole face had been undercut. Following the cutter and resetting supports was probably one of the most dangerous jobs in mining. It was quite common for the machine to 'kick' out from the undercut after hitting something extra hard, knock out the roof supports and cause a roof fall. Or sometimes the coal seam would collapse on top of the No.2 cutterman while he was inserting the temporary supports.

As a cutterman, you were expected to predict the unpredictable, an impossible task since a coal seam rarely went the way you wanted it to. For instance, a small geological fault could occur without any warning, yet you were still expected to maintain the perfect cutting horizon.

On reflection, Prestwick was very fortunate in having cuttermen that were as good as my three cousins. Experience has shown me that their skill and the quality of their work were second to none. George, the youngest of the three brothers, was always full of mischief and forever playing tricks on his workmates. Often he would infuriate Mr Rothery. If he said 'white', George would say 'black'. On one occasion, Mr Rothery got so annoyed that as George was leaving his office, he came running

CUTTING and DRILLING of COAL FACE OPERATION
Working of 24 hour cycle at coal face
(over 5 day week)

Before Face is cut

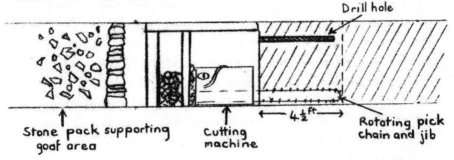

Drill hole

Stone pack supporting goaf area

Cutting machine

$4\frac{1}{2}$ ft

Rotating pick chain and jib

After Face is cut

Coal to be blasted

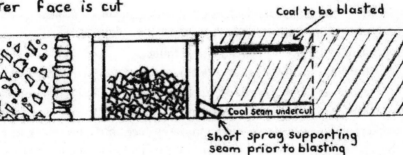

Coal seam undercut

short sprag supporting seam prior to blasting

After coal has been extracted

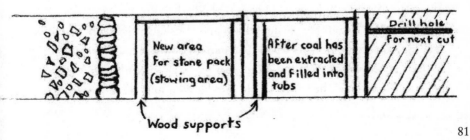

New area for stone pack (stowing area)

After coal has been extracted and filled into tubs

Drill hole for next cut

Wood supports

out after him and shouted 'He who laughs last gathers no bloody moss, or something like that.'

In 1955 the pit head baths were built. To Mam it must have been a great relief; no more boots to clean, clothes to dust or baths to fill every day. Finishing work and being able to take a hot shower was sheer pleasure. After bathing most of the lads would meet in the canteen for a glass of cold milk, having worked and sweated for eight hours, milk tasted like nectar; but there was no substitute for cold water to quench a thirst. As there was no water supply underground, towards the end of the shift spare water was like gold. I've seen men so thirsty that they would give anything for a drink. The older men always seemed to have water left and the younger ones would be so grateful for it.

On rare occasions men would actually steal water from the water bottles of their fellow workers. I can remember one man being so incensed at finding that his water had been stolen that the next day he placed a water bottle that he had filled with urine in a conspicuous place. The culprit didn't steal any more of his water, but the man was reprimanded for doing such a horrible thing.

After finishing my training as a coal-cutter, I was cavilled as a spare filler and found myself working alongside Alec H. Alec lived six miles from the pit in a slum area outside of Newcastle. He wasn't the best of workers and he was always dirty. On the surface, at the beginning of a shift, looking at Alec you would presume he had just completed his shift. He was always black, sweating and tired.

For all his failings, he had a jovial nature and was always kind and helpful. However, he had the annoying habit of forever wiping his top lip and nose with the palm of his hand in an upward movement. And if anyone ever spoke to him, he always replied 'eh?'

Alec loved to gamble on the horses and consequently, never had any money. However, on one occasion, he had a good win and decided to buy himself a new outfit. 'Putting money on me back instead of giving it back to the bookie', he called it. He purchased a new three-piece suit, shirt, tie and underclothes. The following Saturday he was seen standing at the bar of his local dressed in his new outfit, but on his feet he still wore his hob-nailed work boots.

Rumours about conveyors being introduced at Prestwick actually became reality in 1958. The first face conveyor belt was installed in the Busty seam. It was about this time when a pit on the outskirts of Newcastle (the Montague) began to phase down. It eventually closed and some of the workers were transferred to Prestwick. As they were familiar with the conveyor system, several were absorbed into the face team. Others were integrated into the putting and filling teams, which had long been phased out in other pits. The reaction of the transferred miners to this type of work was far from favourable! One of them jokingly compared the work to that carried out by monks, the only difference he could see was that we used boxes on wheels instead of wooden baskets. He wasn't far wrong.

I was sent to work with my cousin Robert on the new face as the manager had decided to split up the brothers. George was sent to cut out a development district in the Brockwell seam. I was No.2 to Robert. Pairs of cuttermen were always referred to as 'one' and 'two'. One was the operator, number two was his second man.

The Busty steam was two feet high, the face ran for 120 yards and was being driven down an incline. The floor was friable while the roof above was made from a very hard sandstone. There were three roadways supplying the main face, as well as a supplies roadway which was also used as a return airway, and a tail roadway which was also used for ferrying supplies. The middle gate was approximately half way between the main-gate and the tail road. In more modern pits it was unusual to have a middle road on a face but the manager thought that the stones produced from firing this roadway could be stowed in the middle of the face, thus giving it more stability.

My job was to help Robert drag the power cable that powered the cutter onto the face and then position the machine alongside the face.

While Robert changed the cutting picks I prepared the tunnel in which the machine was to travel. This meant withdrawing and resetting wood supports, leaving a two feet tunnel through which the machine had to pass. Once the machine began cutting, I began resetting the supports that I had previously altered. It was a skilled job and also highly dangerous.

While working this face I had one of the most frightening experiences of my life underground. The face had been in production for almost 13 weeks and had been turning over one cut a day, advancing steadily at about eight yards a week. For conventional mining this was very good.

The 'goaf' area is the space in an abandoned tunnel and under total extraction mining it normally caves in. However, one particular tunnel was driven through very hard sandstone, and had not collapsed. This left an enormous area of emptiness. When I asked the overman what would happen, he said there was nothing to worry about. According to him, the roof in the 'goaf' area would slowly bend, the floor would rise and eventually they would meet and settle. The overman had been brought to the colliery for his knowledge and experience in conventional mining and was THE authority on such matters. I accepted his theory but remained a little sceptical.

A few days later Robert and I were cutting the coalface. The machine was cutting from the tailroad towards the middle roadway and I was following behind, resetting props and inserting wooden nogs into the undercut. On this occasion the seam was only two feet high and so to do my job I had to lie on my side and snake my way along the tunnel. Suddenly, above the noise of the cutter, I heard a most unusual sound. It was like heavy rain falling on a tin roof. At the same time, flecks of coal dust started to flake off the roof and I could feel them gently hitting my face.

Suddenly there was an almighty sound of thunder and dust clouds appeared everywhere, I couldn't see my hand in front of my face. The

COAL CUTTING OPERATION
Coal face being undercut to a depth of 4½ feet

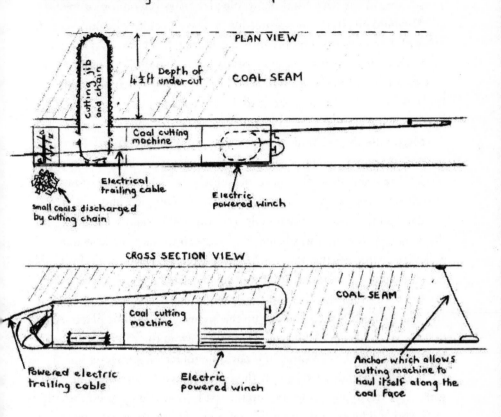

clapping sound of thunder went on and on. As the clouds of dust cleared, I could see Robert in the distance. He was crawling up the face tunnel as fast as he could go. The machine was still cutting merrily along as if nothing had happened.

I was trapped and started to panic. I couldn't crawl back along the tunnel as I was too frightened and yet I couldn't go forward because the machine was in front of me, blocking my way out. And I couldn't get into the conveyor tunnel because it had been blocked off by the small coals that had been churned out by the cutter.

I snuggled up to the machine as close as I could, thinking that if the worst came to the worst and the whole place caved in on top of me, at least I would be given some protection by the machine. The noise eased off for a few seconds, but only to begin again much louder. At the same time I could feel the floor heaving beneath me. I couldn't think for fear, I was so petrified I just started to cry. I have never ever been so frightened. I was convinced that I was about to die – crushed to death by a rumbling earthquake.

Eventually the machine in front of me stopped. In a frenzy I scraped my way through the small coals to make room for myself in the conveyor tunnel. I crawled along the conveyor tunnel past the machine and back into the face tunnel. By now I was in a state of complete shock.

Eventually I reached the middle roadway and I could see Robert in the distance, coming towards me. He had been to the electric switch panels to switch off the power. I had stopped crying by now and was able to stand up in the roadway. Robert grinned at me, 'Are you ...' he didn't get a chance to finish. There was another almighty crack which went on and on. We both turned and ran up the archway. The whole place seemed to come alive, stones of all sizes were falling from the roof and we could hear the steel girders twisting and buckling under the pressure.

I wasn't as frightened now as there was someone with me, but it was still pretty terrifying. As we ran up the roadway we bumped into another man who had been working in the roadway. He was frantically trying to free his jacket that was hanging on a wood prop. 'Never mind your jacket,' I shouted, 'Just get out!' The three of us ran for our lives to reach the roadway entrance. This part of the roadway was supported all round by pillars of coal and we were now in comparative safety.

We all flopped onto the floor breathless. We could still hear the noise as it continued to rattle away in the distance. For a while nobody spoke. A few minutes later I could hear the sound of somebody approaching, it was Mr Rothery. 'What the bloody hell are you doing here?' he enquired. I told him what had happened and after listening intently he replied 'Not frightened of a bit of bloody noise are you?' We had to smile; there was no way anyone would receive sympathy from Mr Rothery. 'Howay then,' he said. 'Get off your bloody arses and lets ganin see what the damage is.'

Robert and I followed him back to the face but the other man refused to come, he wasn't going back there for all the tea in China. In fact he never worked underground again. As we approached the face I noticed that the road tunnel had actually shrunk, the steel arches were all buckled and twisted and wood struts placed between each archway were now broken and sticking out all over the place. The stone packs that had been neatly formed on both sides of the roadway, were now spilling over into it. We could still hear the sound of timber splitting and creaking. The floor of the roadway had lifted and was difficult to walk on.

On reaching the face the first thing I noticed was that the top belt of the conveyor had snapped and was lying on top of the bottom belt. There were sharp edged rocks lying all about the face and on top of the conveyor; this was obviously what had brought down the belt. The further up the face we crawled, the more distorted things became. Wood props, normally two feet high, had been pushed into the floor exposing only half of their height. Steel chocks had been buried and were almost impossible to see. A break several inches wide had formed in the roof and was getting wider and wider the further up the face we crawled.

Near the machine the roof had lowered by some 12 inches. Just past the machine it was impossible to travel any further. However the break in the roof was so large that we could now stand up and look right into it. Shining my light into the large cavity that had been created, I couldn't help but notice the purity of the strata. It was quite awe-inspiring.

Mr Rothery was cursing and swearing even more than usual. It was quite obvious that there would be no production from this face for quite some time. This was borne out the next day by the manager who, after personal inspection, had decided to abandon that half of the face completely. We were instructed to retrieve the cutting machine from where we had abandoned it and cut the other half of the face, which we later did. I always feel somewhat guilty at having cried in that frightening situation, but I am not ashamed. At the time I actually thought I was going to be buried alive.

The face length had been halved and production dropped in proportion. But as this face was now winning out other faces, which would be worked later, things were not as disastrous as had been first envisaged. The face travelled for several hundred yards in its reduced capacity before eventually reaching its boundary.

Shortly afterwards, the manager left Prestwick and returned to his former colliery at North Walbottle. The new manager soon decided that production needed to be increased. The only way this could be achieved was to introduce a third production shift, and this he did. However, this meant creating a third face and a new team of all types of face workers.

I was given the job of No.1 cutter and my partner was to be a man called Alfie. Before starting the job the manager sent for me and explained what he hoped I would achieve. He wanted me to see that the face was cut correctly, that the line was kept straight and see that the production shift got a press button start. In return for this, I could start and finish my shift whenever it was appropriate.

The manager had estimated that there would be around 1,200 tons of coal produced from this face each week. It was up to me whether or not the face would be successful. I was given a brand new cutting machine and I looked after it as if I'd bought it myself. At the end of the cutting operation I would place a plastic cover over the whole length of the cutting machine to keep out any water or dust. I also oiled and greased the chain regularly.

The face was a tremendous success, lasting over two years and seldom missing a cut. It advanced around 1,200 yards. Alfie and I made fantastic money, it was close to £2,000 a year or £40 per week. In 1960 this was well over double the national average which was twice as much as a First Division professional footballer earned. I was the only one of my mates who could afford a car, and a brand new one at that.

It was around this time in the fifties that Prestwick Colliery had a football team in the amateur league. At 14 years of age and still at school I played my first game for the team as they were short of a player. We were playing against Sigmund Pumps, a North East mining equipment firm. We were losing 2-1 when I scored, making it two all at half time. We went on to win 4-2, and my feelings were such that you would have thought I had scored at Wembley!

Work and football both required physical effort and because of all the football injuries the colliery manager could not run his colliery with absenteeism, or as he described it 'sick notes'. So, in later years when I became a 'key' worker, I was told by the manager to 'pack the football in'. The team eventually folded because of management pressure.

The only time the face missed a daily cut was when I had taken a week's leave of absence for my honeymoon. Alfie, who took over the controls when I was away, made a right mess of cutting the face. Instead of keeping the jib on the floor of the seam, he allowed it to ride up, thus losing height and leaving coal underneath, so much so in fact that it had to be re-drilled and fired. Apparently he'd panicked after a small mechanical breakdown and cut the face too quickly without taking proper care and attention. He later confessed to detesting being on the 'handles' and was much happier being the No.2.

Alfie was a bachelor in his late forties who lived with his elderly mother. His main aim in life was to consume as much beer as humanly possible; it was very rare for him to miss a session at his local. He drank Newcastle Brown Ale as if it was going out of fashion, downing eight pints at lunchtime and the same at night, depending on his shift. On his annual holidays he would visit small villages in Northumberland; he wanted to be able to boast that he'd drunk a pint of beer in every public house in the county. He never did achieve this goal, but eventually died in the process.

On some occasions he got so drunk that he ended up in hospital (known locally as the Brown Ale ward). His doctor warned him what would happen if he continued to drink so much and told him that if he didn't stop he'd be dead within six months. For a while he took this advice, consuming only two pints of ordinary beer a day. Alfie reckoned this was moderation enough. However he shortly returned to his bad habits and died within a few months.

Alfie and I worked together for almost five years, and in that time he was very loyal to me, following whatever I'd decided. It was up to me to say what time we started our shift and often I'd have to seek him from his home if there was no transport. We usually started in the early hours of the morning and the smell of drink on his breath was enough to intoxicate me. I would ask him if he was alright and he would give me his usual reply, which was 'I'll be alreet as soon as a get a sweat on.' And he usually was!

On one occasion we were half way along the face with the machine cutting away from the main road. Alfie, as usual, was following behind doing the timber work. I was in the process of slackening off the steel haulage rope when, above the sound of the machine I heard Alfie cry out. Looking up I saw him sitting on top of the small coals with his back against a wood prop and his two feet side by side sticking out into the coalface. 'What's wrong?' I asked. He didn't reply, he just kept shouting 'That's bloody champion. That's bloody champion that is.' It soon became clear to me what he was doing in this position with his two feet together, he was comparing their length; a third of his left foot had just been severed. The steel toe cap of his safety boot was missing, as well as that part of his boot and his foot.

Examining his foot, I could see small bones, as thick as match sticks, sticking out from what was left of his boot. His big toe, and the three toes next to it had been completely cut off. However, there was very little blood and he appeared to be in no pain. 'How the bloody hell did you do that?' I asked. He didn't reply.

It was then I noticed that the guard covering the machine end of the jib was missing. As soon as I saw this I realised what had happened.

Normally Alfie would crawl along the conveyor tunnel when the machine reached its anchor stay, but on this occasion, because the seam was about three-and-a-half feet high, he decided that there was enough room for him crawl over the top of the machine. As he placed his left knee on top of the machine, he foot dangling over the side. It fell into the rotating steel worm in a moment of sheer carelessness. The steel toe cap of his foot was sliced off by the worm, like a knife cutting into soft butter.

Here we were, almost trapped in the narrow tunnel of the coal seam which, due to the operation of the cutter, was now almost full to capacity with small coals, making it physically impossible for me to drag him to the main roadway which was some 60 yards away. And from there it was at least two miles to the shaft. The deputy had already left the district and by now he would be in the vicinity of the shaft, waiting to be relieved by his 'marra', the oncoming deputy. The nearest phone was half a mile away at the main roadway entrance. I felt completely deserted.

I knew that the face conveyor belt had already been tested and was ready for production. My main aim was to get Alfie off the face as quickly as possible. 'Lie on the belt,' I told him, 'and I'll crawl along to the main roadway and get the belt going, to give you a ride off.'

After getting him off the face I helped him to the place where our clothes were kept. I sat him down and tore up my top shirt to tie around Alfie's boot, at least this would keep out the muck and the dust. I then helped him to put on his shirt and jacket. 'Sit there with your foot up while I go to the phone and get help.' 'Don't panic', said Alfie, 'I'm alright, I'll follow you out.'

As I made my way to the telephone I looked behind me to see Alfie's light in the distance, he was hobbling along trying to catch up. Eventually I reached the phone and informed Mr Rothery. I told him what I'd done and asked him to arrange for us to be transported from the tub loading point to the bottom of the shaft, and then to ring for an ambulance.

I went back towards the face and by now Alfie was almost half way along the main roadway. I helped him to reach the tub loading point, by which time Mr Rothery had lowered an empty set of tubs down the incline from the shaft. Alfie and I each got into an empty tub and were hauled to the shaft bottom. It was illegal to ride in the empty tubs but under the circumstances who cared?

After getting Alfie to the surface and into the awaiting ambulance, I had to return to the face and carry on with the cutting operation. The next day an inquiry was held in the colliery manager's office to discover why the accident had occurred. I explained that it was quite common for the steel worm to lose its guard when the machine stalled, or for it to be dislodged when the direction of the cutting chain was reversed. This explanation seemed to satisfy the manager and the safety officer and in future, all guards were to be welded on to the machine to prevent similar accidents. Alfie returned to work after a two-month lay-off (on the grass, as he called it), minus his toes.

By now (1962) Prestwick had become a highly efficient modern mine producing more than 2,500 tons of coal in a week, more than double its previous target. The coal drawing facilities of the shaft winding system were at full capacity. The surface layout had also been mechanised, taking much of the manpower out of handling tubs on the surface.

At the face though, physical graft was still required to shovel the coals into the conveyor belt. But efforts were being made to eliminate this task. A North-East firm, Huwood, introduced the first power-loading machine to Prestwick. It was known locally as the 'sky-hi'. The face still had to be cut out with the cutting machine but then the 'sky-hi' would (theoretically) load the coals onto the conveyor belt after they had been drilled and fired. It was partially successful for a few weeks, but it never reduced the manpower of the face team as was first thought.

The group of collieries in south Northumberland had a league table to compare production from the 'sky-hi'. I vividly remember the production deputy on the 'sky-hi' face at Prestwick, being congratulated by the area manager because his face became top of the league table.

Little did the manager know that the 'sky-hi' had been taken off the face and production went back to hand-filling! It was typical of the way management operated, the way things appeared to have been done was more important than what was actually being done.

This was a very exciting era at Prestwick. The colliery full of hustle and bustle and everyone seemed happy. I was told in confidence by the NUM secretary that in the first half of the financial year the two pits had made half a million pounds profit.

The pace of things at the colliery was always very fast; everything and everyone was geared to production and there had been no major fatalities or accidents. Because it was a small unit, working at the colliery was like being part of a family.

The first thing I did on getting out of bed, having worked the night-shift, was to ask Mam how the pit had been performing that day. She could tell by the constant banging of the cages as they reached the surface or the squeaking of the conveyors as they carried coals to the screening sheds, whether or not there had been a good day's production. If production ceased at all there was an unusual stillness in the air, just like there was on Sundays.

If production stopped for some time, there would be a sense of uneasiness among the women in the terrace. They worried that someone may have been injured or even killed. Men walking up the back alleyway from the pit to the bus stop would be questioned to discover what had gone wrong. Had a set of tubs been derailed or had there been a power failure? Their minds would be set at ease. They always seemed to prepare themselves for the worst. Perhaps it was a reaction which had been handed down through the generations.

Sunday was usually the day on which union meetings were held. They took place in the pit canteen once a fortnight. At one meeting there were only 11 members present and I found myself elected to the General Committee. Mam didn't like me being in the union and I certainly didn't want to be a committee man. However, I was finally persuaded to join the committee by the secretary. That led to me becoming a member of the Colliery Consultative Council whose function was to review all aspects of mining relative to the colliery.

I learned from one of these meetings that the colliery had 20 years of life left at the present rate of extraction and production. Provided we drove two underground drifts through the 20 feet fault in the Brockwell seam, we should have an area of approximately one square mile of coal to extract. There was a drift mine called the Havannah with a face already approaching from the other side of the fault and heading towards us. It was feared that if they reached this area first it would further reduce the life of Prestwick.

The two drifts at Prestwick eventually reached the coal reserves and we then developed the area. I cannot remember a happier time in the whole of my working life. Every person put the pit first and this created a cheerful working environment.

In the mid-sixties, after the Beeching report closed many railway lines, it was rumoured that both Prestwick and East Walbottle collieries would have to close. Workers would be transferred to the Havannah drift mine which was about a mile away (as the crow flies). It employed about 600 men. But earnings at the Havannah were almost half those at Prestwick, so you can imagine how the men felt on hearing this prospect. However, as this was not scheduled to happen for at least two years, there was ample time for discussion.

It was during this period that Jimmy M., the world champion coal filler from East Walbottle, came to work at Prestwick. One Sunday night in July, during the first shift of the week, dressed in only short trousers, a vest and knee pads, and working in a three feet, three inch seam, Jimmy hand-filled 55 tons of coal. Five shifts and 40 working hours later, he walked out of East Walbottle pit on the outskirts of Dinnington with a record that was to make him a legend in the industry. In that week, working on his knees, he hand filled a mind-boggling 280 tons of coal. It has remained a world record to this day and is likely to remain a permanent entry in the Guinness Book of Records.

This feat earned him the princely sum of £29, plus 48 pounds of soap from a well-known Tyneside manufacturer. He also received a letter from the chairman of the northern division of the NCB which read:

The Board has asked me to convey to you their thanks for your splendid work and example which rebounds not only to your personal credit, but does so much to enhance the reputation of the mining community at a time when critics are not lacking.

Jimmy, to his credit, is the first to pay tribute to the man who putted for him that day. That man was John F. (Dad's cousin), another Dinnington resident that still lives in the village. To keep Jimmy supplied he had to put 90 tubs a day!

Even before that record-breaking week, Jimmy M. had made his mark in mining. As a congratulatory letter from the Coal Board pointed out, in the calendar year up to July he had produced an amazing 3,589 tons of coal. It was a truly amazing feat. However, it was just as well that Jimmy set that record when he did. A few months later, a car came around a bend on the wrong side of the road and collided with his motor cycle. He was off work for six months while surgeons painstakingly tried to remove fragments of glass from his knee.

Unfortunately they couldn't remove all of the glass and from then on Jimmy was never able to kneel and fill coal at the face. There is still glass in his knee today and it is permanently swollen. Jimmy eventually became a deputy and served the rest of his time in mining deputising at East Walbottle, Prestwick and Havannah.

4 Getting on in the world

I have always thought that people do not generally give enough credit to manual workers and the people that supervise them. When I started my deputy's training I soon learned exactly how much skill and responsibility it requires to work underground.

In 1964, with a wife and baby daughter to support and knowing that the high earnings I made at piece-work rates at Prestwick would eventually cease, I decided it was time to think about the future. By now I had experienced every type of conventional mining – face work, coal filling, drilling, making and preparing roadways, advancing conveyors, cutting the face, composite work, operating underground haulage and transport machinery, building junctions, laying track, assisting in driving drifts and staples (a vertical shaft between two seams), and re-modelling roadways. My next step was to apply for a place on the next Potential Deputy's Course.

The interview was held at the Northern Group's Area Offices. There was a panel of six interviewers who asked me why I wanted to become a deputy; what, in my opinion, was the deputy's job; how I would react in certain situations, and so on. At the end of the interview I was told not to be too disappointed if I didn't get a place on the course as there were only 20 places for the 120 applicants.

The week before the course was due to start, I still hadn't heard anything and I was sure I had failed. However, on Friday I was summoned to the manager's office and told to be at Ashington Technical College for nine o'clock on Monday. I felt so proud.

My two elder brothers were now both deputies at Prestwick and I thought that whatever they could do I could do as well. There were over

40 collieries in Northumberland in 1964 and to get a place on the deputy's course was sure to lead to job security, or so I thought.

The course lasted 13 weeks. Six whole weeks were spent at the technical college. After that we studied at the college for two days a week and spent a further two days at a colliery getting practical experience. We also visited colliery workshops and mining machinery firms. I was assigned to Havannah Colliery for my practical experience which was fortunate because it eventually merged with Prestwick.

A deputy is an official of the mine, appointed by the manager to be in charge of a district underground. He is in charge of all the workmen in that district and of all the operations carried out by them. That involves carrying out the manager's instructions, ensuring that the men work in safe conditions, as governed by various Acts of Parliament, and running the district as efficiently and economically as possible.

As the course progressed I began to realise what I had let myself in for. The amount of information I had to digest was mind-boggling.

One of the deputy's main responsibilities is health and safety in his district. At the beginning and end of each shift he must make inspections of his district and write a report on the presence of gas, ventilation, supports and general safety.

A deputy must also make sure that the men in his district follow rules and do nothing that would endanger safety. If an accident does occur, he must make sure that injured men are treated and take charge of any recovery operations as well as producing a report, measurements and a sketch map of the incident.

One of the primary objects of the course was to learn all about mine gases and how to detect them. Airborne dust is another major health hazard underground because it is highly explosive. Although most of the major mining explosions were started by an ignition of methane gas they developed into coal dust explosions. It is part of the deputy's job to make sure that all possible precautions against fire and explosions are taken.

A deputy needs a shot firing certificate, which means learning how to stem and fire shot holes, understand the amounts and type of explosives required and knowing all the explosives regulations.

On the course we were also taught how to deploy men and ensure that every man is trained correctly for the job he is doing.

At the end of the course 19 of us were successful, one failed. My head was now stuffed with regulations. As the lad who failed said, 'It's bloody university professors they want, not deputies.'

Being a deputy in charge of an underground district is like having a village where you are the policeman, the doctor, the fireman, the priest, the schoolmaster, the bank manager, Uncle Tom Cobbley and ruler of all. Police have no jurisdiction underground, deputies are governed by an Act of Parliament (Mines and Quarries Act, 1954). In a typical eight-hour shift you are responsible for the work and safety of up to 50 men working along a two-mile roadway and on a face of up to 250 yards long. A deputy is also responsible for any other workers or visitors who arrive in his district during the shift.

I returned to Prestwick armed with my Deputy's Certificate, shot-firing certificate, gas and hearing certificate and first aid certificate. The manager, congratulated me on my success and, with a big grin on his face, said 'You'll have forgotten most of it in a fortnight.' Funny comment to make, I thought at the time.

In 1965 Prestwick merged with the Havannah drift mine. Coals ceased to be sent up the Prestwick shaft, they were now conveyed out via one of the two underground roads which linked the pits together. However, workmen at Prestwick still used their old shaft and pit head baths and worked the old coalfaces on piece-work rates. But when the Brockwell and Busty seams had been worked out, Prestwick Colliery was abandoned and all underground workings were now headed at Havannah. In 1966 both Prestwick and East Walbottle Collieries closed and men were transferred to Havannah.

Twelve months before East Walbottle closed, at the height of the

Asian flu epidemic, I was sent to work there as an official. Although I was a qualified deputy I was still a member of the NUM and not a member of the officials' union (the National Association of Colliery Overmen, Deputies and Shot-firers). This was because officials at East Walbottle and Prestwick had not yet been guaranteed a job at the Havannah.

Coal at East Walbottle was still being hand-filled and hand-putted using the board and pillar system where pillars of coal remained as supports. Just under 200 men worked at East Walbottle, and like Prestwick, it was obviously a happy little pit and a great one to work in. It was probably the most efficient and profitable colliery in the county, and I could see now why both collieries made profits; everyone put the pit first, their loyalty was second to none. I felt proud to have worked at East Walbottle, even though it had only been for a few weeks.

Prestwick Colliery and East Walbottle Colliery both closed in 1966, taking with them the remains of the Victorian era of coal mining.

5 Havannah – taking risks

Havannah was opened in 1952 as a short-term project, to provide employment for workers from the four Throckley collieries, Maria, Isabella, Coronation and Blucher, which were closing. It had an estimated life of 15 years but it didn't close until 1976, when it was no longer economic. It ran due east from Newcastle airport and some of its workings were actually underneath the runway.

At its peak Havannah produced half a million tons a year and employed almost 1,000 men. It was the first day-wage pit in the country and the workmen had to clock on and off like the workmen in a factory.

The surface buildings were surrounded by lush green lawns and pretty rose borders. The covered buildings were so well laid out that passers-by would never have recognised it as a coal mine. Because it was a drift mine it had no shaft or cage and you could walk in and out of the mine without having to be lowered mechanically underground.

Coals were conveyed to the surface by a cable belt, which was a conveyor suspended across two parallel steel wire ropes. It travelled almost the whole length of the intake shaft, which was just over half a mile long, and was capable of carrying 300 tons of coal an hour. It was controlled from the surface, as were most of the underground conveyors. This system was the envy of all collieries and its installation cost was estimated at well over £30,000.

The conveyor system was so efficient that I can remember at one time nine separate conveyors being controlled by one patrol man. Each conveyor had its own pre-start warning device: before it started up, a loud klaxon horn sounded, frightening the living day lights out of you if you happened to be passing by at the time.

Havannah had gone through a purple patch in the early sixties as a result of its highly mechanised plough faces in the low main seams and for a time it was almost 100 per cent mechanised. But when Havannah merged with Prestwick all the good faces had been worked out and conventional methods were used again. The cream had gone.

For the workmen from Prestwick the transfer had been very smooth, largely due to the fact that most of the face workers were still working in the same place, the only difference being that they had to travel to the face via Havannah instead of Prestwick. For me there was no problem at all as I had spent two days a week over a three-month period on the Deputy's Course at Havannah, and I had got to know the place extremely well.

At first you could sense some friction between the Havannah workers and the men from Prestwick. One of the reasons was that the men from Prestwick were still on piece-work rates and so earning a much bigger wage. But as time went by, moods changed and everyone became friends.

In January 1967 I was summoned to the colliery manager's office and asked to explain why I was not a member of NACODS – the officials' union. I was still being paid at my average piece rates, £5 more than the officials, as I was still a member of the NUM. A week later I was transferred from the NUM to NACODS and was now a deputy of the mine.

At first I was a Grade II Deputy, the shot-firer. My job was to stem all the shot-holes that had been drilled on the coalface and fire them. For this I carried 60 instantaneous detonators in a box strapped to my waist.

The shift at the face was approximately six hours and by law I was supposed to fire ten shots per hour, but this never worked in practice. The shot firers fired their shots to suit the workmen's requirements and for the good of face production. After all, we were there for one purpose and that was to produce coal. Over the years I have seen so many stupid things done regarding shot-firing regulations that if I put it in writing I would probably end up in the Tower of London, beheaded. The two greatest attributes that an official underground must possess are common sense and a sense of humour; take these two factors away and you are worthless.

The face was producing over 200 tons per day and almost 1,100 tons per week. This was above the average for conventional mining, and one of the techniques used was prop-free front support system. Cantilever action provided roof support up to the coalface leaving a space free from vertical supports between the waste side of the conveyor and the face. There was room for a power loader to operate and for the face conveyor to be pushed up to the face without having to dismantle it.

Various types of props and steel bars were introduced with some degree of success, but it wasn't until the Powered Roof Support hydraulic chock, with a cantilever-type roof support was introduced, that mechanisation of the coalface really took off. These types of supports, coupled by hydraulic rams to a steel armoured flexible face conveyor, were the solution to modern mining, the beginning of continuous mining and the end of the pick and shovel era.

Plans were drawn to install and equip a 200-yard advancing face at the Prestwick workings of Havannah, in the four foot Brockwell seam, using the new type of supports and armoured flexible conveyors (AFC). The coal-getting machine was to be a conveyor-mounted trepan shearer, a completely new invention.

So new was the machine that men and officials were sent to the manufacturer to be trained how to use it. It was decided to produce coals in two shifts a day and to work and advance the roadways (gates) in the same shift as production. This was a major breakthrough in mining; on conventional faces production was usually confined to one shift per day and preparation was carried out on the other shifts. The new system introduced continuous mining.

The new powered roof supports (chocks) were brought underground via the Prestwick shaft and transported on their own wheels, which had been specially prepared for them. My first impression on seeing them installed on the face was sheer delight, a line of steel from end to end, all along the face. With this type of support there would never be a roof fall on the face again (or so I thought).

Two face teams were deployed to the new face. One team consisted of workmen from Prestwick, the other was made up with men from the Havannah. The Coal Board had also introduced a number of specialised workmen to assist in the face operations. These men were members of the mechanisation department and known as the 'mech team'. They would travel from pit to pit, assisting in the introduction of mechanisation. They were originally officials from pits in the area and were hand picked for their ability and common sense.

This trepan shearer cored out the centre of the coal seam and produced a large coal suitable for the household market. It was a monster of a machine, 22 feet in length with an overhead turret jib and two pre-cutting jibs. It hauled itself along a steel chain which was anchored at both ends of the armoured face conveyor.

Apart from a few weeks of average production the 'face' turned out to be a disaster. The new powered supports were absolutely useless because their base was too narrow, causing them to fall over when they were being advanced. This had a domino effect, knocking several over at once and exposing the roof, creating falls and presenting a new dimension in mining, the timbering of roof cavities. The four-feet-thick Brockwell seam also became thinner and, as the turret jib of the trepan shearer was not designed to cut the hard sandstone roof, it was impossible for it to work.

Not having proper supports, the machine was unable to cut and load the coal as the seam was too narrow and so it was eventually closed; all chocks were lost and left abandoned. It was my first taste of mechanisation and although it had failed, it was a good education for the future.

It was around this time that I was sent as a deputy to the Havannah side of the pit to take charge of a hand-filling conventional district in the production shift. I noticed that the general pace of the men and fellow officials was much more relaxed and slower, in some instances it was almost pathetic. For every man hand filling at Prestwick, the ratio at Havannah was approximately one-and-a-half. For example, on a 120 yard face, three feet high in the Brockwell seam, it would take eight men to fill off all the coals. At the Havannah it would take 12 men! The workmen didn't kill themselves and their slogan was a fair day's work for a fair day's pay.

Being used to the piece-work system, I found it difficult to accept this slower pace. The men took an immediate dislike to me as I was always trying to push them, they thought, too hard.

My second observation was the general lack of efficiency in the district. I had been taught that the first hour of a production shift was vital. Everything must be ready for the workman to start filling coals as soon as he arrived at the face at the beginning of his shift (a push button start was the term we used locally).

When I was coal cutting, after completing the cutting of the face, I would make sure the tensioning of the face conveyor was as it should be, and that there were no obstructions in the conveyor belt tunnel. Before leaving the district at the end of my shift, I would give the face conveyor a run, making sure everything was ready for coal work to begin immediately.

At Havannah I found that quite often the conveyor was under-tensioned and the cutting operation had not been completed, which would waste a couple of hours before production began. This meant that at the end of the production shift, half the face still had to be filled off. More men had to be deployed on the following shift to complete it. It also meant that the workmen who made the roadways lost half a shift because they were unable to get on with their own work, so more men had to be deployed to complete the roadways. Where it took two men to cut the face at Prestwick, it sometimes took four men at Havannah, and very rarely was it completed in a single shift.

The result was that there were four cycles of production instead of five. At Prestwick, the loss of a cycle (or face cut) was unheard of. Some of the Havannah face workers (especially the older ones) worked at a piece-work rate as they had been accustomed to this method at their parent colliery, before they came to the Havannah. It was mainly the younger workers who had never done piece-work that had a 'couldn't care less attitude'.

It is probably wrong of me to make comparisons between the Prestwick workers and the Havannah ones as, on reflection, the Prestwick men were the nearest thing to super-human that you could get in the mining industry.

It was while I was working at the Havannah side of the pit on the conventional faces that I had another frightening experience that I shall never forget. It was almost at the end of the filling shift and I was on a statutory pre-shift inspection. I was also checking to see how much coal there was left to fill off for the oncoming shift. It was getting late and all the men were off the face in the roadways, preparing to go home. I had started to crawl from the tail-gate roadway and was making my way down the three-feet-high face towards the main-gate roadway. There were stooks of coal left at various intervals along the face. To get past these stooks of coal I had to crawl onto the face conveyor belt.

For no reason whatsoever, and without warning, the conveyor started up. Although it was illegal to ride it, it was common practice along the face and as there was no one there to see me the temptation was too great. I was riding along in a kneeling position when all of a sudden the whole area of goaf (waste) collapsed. The accompanying rush of air was so strong that it turned me over in a complete somersault. I lost my flame safety lamp. My hat and cap lamp came off my head and I was on my back on a moving conveyor in complete darkness.

By now I had my electric lamp lit and was holding it in my hand. It took several minutes for the ventilation to clear the airborne dust. I was covered from head to foot in dust and as black as the ace of spades.

The large stone had broken off by the row of face chocks which is what they were designed to do. The face tunnel and conveyor tunnel were intact. The stone had fallen in the large expanse of emptiness in the waste area.

When I eventually reached the drift bottom and was waiting in the mine cars to be hauled to the surface, I began to tell my fellow officials of my experience. They all laughed and thought it had been a huge joke and told me I shouldn't have been riding on the face conveyor belt in the first place.

It was decided to install and equip a new mechanised face unit at Prestwick to run alongside the face that had been abandoned. It was to be supported with the most modern chocks available at the time, and would have two machine shearers on the face. One would be at the tail end of the face to cut one fifth of the face. It would eliminate the tailgate stall, thus saving time and manpower. The other main machine would cut and load four fifths of the face.

I was chosen to be deputy in charge of one of the two production shifts. I was very excited and happy at the prospect, for I was about to take charge of a highly mechanised district, with the most advanced and sophisticated machinery in the country.

A deputy's job was primarily concerned with safety. On starting work in a new district there were many things to do to such as learning the boundaries of the district, locating the two ways out to the surface, looking at the plans, records of ventilation, firedamp measurements and any special features such as methane drainage and prevention work. I also had to make a mental note of the position of telephones, first aid containers, morphia safes and fire fighting appliances. It was essential to know what each individual workman did and make sure he was trained and authorised to do it and talk to the men and let them know what we, as a team, were trying to achieve. By law a deputy had to make a pre-shift inspection during his shift, but some collieries have different systems. The best system I found was to make my own pre-shift

Temporary Support

Chock

Conveyor belt empty

Conveyor belt with coal

Handfilling conveyor

When all coal cleared conveyor belt moved across → → →

Previous rock collapses after chock supports advanced to new track

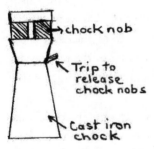

→ chock nob

← Trip to release chock nobs

← Cast iron chock

Cast iron chock used to support roof then released and moved as required to next track

inspection, that way I could give information to the workmen first hand. Using the other system you relied on the word of the out going deputy. It was incredible how the state and position of a district varied between what you saw and what you had been told!

Deploying men to their work at the beginning of a shift was usually

107

a straightforward job, because on a mechanised unit men normally knew exactly what their jobs were and where they were working. An official's job was to determine the priorities and deploy the men accordingly. A deputy had to record all the names of workmen in his district including non-colliery personnel.

A district cannot function efficiently without a regular supply of materials. As a deputy, I had to make sure that no delays were caused by shortages and inform a senior official (overman or under-manager) before supplies got too low. Unloading and stacking the materials was important underground, as a lot of accidents were caused by untidiness. As a deputy I had to set high standards at the beginning so the men on supplies knew what to expect from me.

One of the biggest improvements in mining at that time was the communications system. It became possible to contact other districts and even the colliery manager's office or engineer's office at the surface. Just by pushing a button on an eight-inch box you could contact the control operator at the surface and he could put you through to any face, district pumping station, roadway, mechanical or electrical department, in fact, almost anywhere in the colliery. These boxes were placed at intervals along the face and attached to the powered supports. You were never more than ten yards away from a phone. Tannoys were placed at 200-yard intervals along the two roadway tunnels leading to the face so if someone was trying to contact you, it was virtually impossible for you not to hear.

The system used on conventional coalfaces was a one-piece telephone at each end of the face. You spoke into the mouth piece and used the same mouth piece for listening. After speaking into the phone you then placed it against your ear to receive the message. It was frustrating because at times you should have been listening instead of speaking and sometimes when speaking you would be holding the mouthpiece against your ear, it was quite hilarious at times.

Even that one-piece phone system was an improvement on the

previous one which was to pass verbal messages via individual workmen along the face. For instance, if a workman wanted some supports from the tail-gate supplies road, he shouted to the next workmen who was approximately 12 yards down the face, he in turn passed on the message to the next man and so on until word reached the supply men at the tail end of the face. If the original message was six three-foot wood props and three wood planks, it would probably end up as six wood planks and three six-foot wood props!

These supports would then be placed onto the face belt and transported along the face. If one of the six-foot props rolled off and lodged itself across the belt it would cause an obstruction and a build up of coals, which led to overloading and caused the belt to snap and break. This simple mistake could lead to a delay of at least two hours production. Farcical situations like this often happened, and a substantial loss in output occurred.

Another big improvement was the transportation of men from the surface to the coalface and back again. Men were lowered down and hauled up the main intake drift in mine cars, 24 per car in a train of six cars, totalling 140 men at a time. On arriving at the drift bottom they continued by man-riding conveyors along various roadways, eventually arriving within 100 yards of the face. They rode on the bottom belt going to the face and on the top belt returning to the drift bottom.

Proper boarding platforms were made to get on to the moving conveyors and alighting platforms for getting off. All sorts of rules and regulations were introduced to stop people from abusing the system. It's ironic though – at one time, men were fined for riding on conveyors underground but were now being asked to use them to speed up the journey to and from the face. That, I suppose, is progress.

Unknown to me at the time, highly mechanised faces were being introduced throughout the country; they were known as 'Spear head' faces. Apparently they were the brainchild of Lord Robens who was then the chairman of the NCB. In 1967 Lord Robens visited several coalfields in America to see first-hand the performance of British-made machines at work in the American mines. On his return he sent a letter to all 15 area directors, stating that each director should have at least one coalface in his area that produced 1,000 tons per day.

'He must be bloody crackers!' was my first thought when I heard of the plan. 'Impossible!' I started to visualise what it would take to produce that amount and could it be achieved on my face. For a coalface to produce 1,000 saleable tonnage, it would have to be 225 yards long, three-and-a-half feet high and the depth of cut would have to be 27 inches. Each cut would produce an estimated 198 tons. As my face was 25 yards shorter than this, it meant that six cuts or strips per day would have to be achieved to reach the magical figure of 1,000 tons.

So, a five-day week's production of 5,000 tons would take 30 strips or cuts, and as the face had two production shifts per day, that made three strips per shift. The length of working time available during a shift at the face was approximately six hours, so each cut had to take not more than two hours. That meant the machine had to cut the face from the main roadway, along its length and then return to the main road end on the ploughing run. The machine had to travel up and down the face to complete one shearer strip. Perhaps it was not an impossible task after all. After initial teething problems the face started to get better and better results. There was a friendly competition between the shifts of workmen and officials, when one shift achieved two shears per shift, the second shift eventually achieved the same. Gradually both shifts achieved the necessary three shears per shift and the magic figure of 1,000 tons per day. I realised that production from one face in a day was the equivalent of a full week's production when I first started mining at Prestwick in 1953. That was indeed progress.

The first mine to achieve Lord Robens' 1,000-ton target was Longhirst Drift mine, also in Northumberland. I was very disappointed when I heard we had just been pipped at the post, especially as the Coal Board later made a film to commemorate the occasion. The film was eventually shown in all of the coalfields throughout Britain.

It was a really exciting time. I actually enjoyed the work, the friendliness, the competition, the whole atmosphere. It was a pleasure to be part of it. I was so keen to produce coal that when I was underground, all alone during a pre-shift inspection, I would sometimes prepare a cutting machine for a straight start. This sometimes entailed advancing the face conveyor, moving forward and resetting the hydraulic supports, and even operating the machine. It was a marvellous and stimulating feeling – you really felt as if you belonged. On reflection it was probably a stupid thing to do, but as all of the conveyors were controlled at the surface I had no thought of danger at. Here was I, all alone underground, producing tons of coal.

To me, seeing an underground conveyor loaded to capacity with coals and winding its way along the tunnel, the tunnel straight and the line of conveyor graded and aligned to perfection, was a thing of beauty.

I found out very early that mechanised districts required the same principles as a conventional district. By that I mean roadways and faces must be kept straight and to the correct grade and line. Cheating and taking short cuts never worked. Producing coal at one end of the face because the preparation had not been done at the other end was alright in the short term, but not in the long term. I am a great believer in taking orders from the situation. If something is wrong, I have never been afraid to stop it and put it right. Leaving a situation to be put right by your opposite number in the other shift, works some of the time, but much depends on personal relationships, and the strength and character of the under-manager who is in overall charge of the districts. Leaving things to be put right tomorrow never really works.

At Havannah the simple job of putting a straight white line on the roof along the entire length of the face once a week and then bringing the hydraulic powered supports and the face conveyor onto this line could make the difference between working in good conditions or terrible ones. Not only did it bring all the supports into line, it also helped to take the tension and undulations out from armoured flexible conveyors. The cutting machine, which mounted and traversed the conveyor, relied on the conveyor to be level in relation to the gradient of the seam. If the conveyor became uneven the cutting machine disc would push through the top of the seam and expose the strata above. Once this happened, the friable nature of the strata would break up and cause a roof fall and expose a cavity above the powered supports. This often made working conditions dangerous and led to a delay in production.

The introduction of mechanisation and the prop-free front system brought a new dimension into timbering large cavities caused by roof falls. Old wood railway sleepers were used, built in layers on top of each other like a trellis and set so they would span three powered supports. Sometimes the cavities were so high and large that it was impossible to support them right up to the roof. When this occurred a false roof was created on top of the powered supports by laying wood sleepers parallel to each other. This prevented more of the roof from flushing in.

One cavity became so large that production was stopped for several weeks. Stones were continually falling (luckily) straight onto the face conveyor. It was so dangerous that the workmen refused to go into the cavity area and support it so it was left to the officials of the district. We eventually got all the hydraulic supports moved forward and a false roof created. As soon as we had completed the job more stones fell and kept falling, but were unable to penetrate the false roof.

The production manager was so worried that he decided to postpone production until after the annual holidays, which were two days away. In fact, he was so concerned that he was thinking of abandoning it as a production unit.

The dictionary says a cavity is a hole of any size, well, I suppose there are cavities and cavities. This particular one was so large that when standing in the middle of it, you were unable to see the roof, even with the aid of a spot light. Remember, the face hadn't advanced for several weeks due to the almost continuous falling of stones. The roof above the goaf (or waste area) had moved back, away from the face and formed a large crevice which gave it the appearance of the side of a gigantic mountain (length of fall 40 feet long by 12 feet wide).

The first production shift after the holidays was to start at 12.30am on Monday. Being the deputy in charge, I started at 11.30 pm, one hour earlier, to make a pre-shift inspection. Knowing that the face hadn't moved for several weeks, I suspected I'd be in for a rough shift.

As I crawled along the face, I passed the fall area without realising it. I crawled back and took a more detailed look. It was impossible to see into the cavity area as the false roof had done its job, and there were tons of stones lying on top of it. I made several examinations, crawling back and forward looking for potential falls that might occur once the machine had eventually cut through it.

I decided that the fall area appeared to be well secured. So, with a little bit of luck and some precautions in the fall area, maybe we could get the face back to normal and good production.

After testing for gas I finished my inspection and returned to the meeting station in time for the arrival of the workmen. I informed the men and the overman of my plan, and they appeared to be very sceptical about my enthusiasm.

I instructed the two machine operators to cut through the fall area and then place the machine just outside of the fall area ready to cut it again once we had advanced and secured the conveyor and supports. I ordered the power to be disconnected from the machine and the conveyor, as quiet is essential when working in dangerous conditions. In mining you have to hear what you are doing, as well as see. Then, activating the hydraulic rams which slowly pushed forward the armoured flexible face conveyor into the track left by the cutting machine, we proceeded to advance, one by one, the 13 powered supports that spanned the fall area. Twelve of the supports came without much difficulty, but the 13th, right slap bang in the middle of the fall area, seemed to be stuck. 'Who's going to get that one?' I thought. No one else made any attempt to advance it. It is in situations like this when you had to lead from the front. 'Everyone get back' I shouted, 'clear the fall area.' I didn't want too many bodies in the way in case things went wrong. After all, there was a cavity of unknown dimensions immediately above and gigantic stones might rain down at any moment.

I tried to use the support's operating handle several times but nothing happened. After a more detailed examination I saw the reason why the support wouldn't lower, it was jammed fast against the wood rail sleeper of the false roof. I needed someone to operate the support in the lower position while I physically forced the support down. Bill S., the overman, duly obliged. So I placed the metal mouth of a flat, round shovel between the top of the hydraulic powered support and the wooden sleeper. Using the shovel as a lever, I forced the support to lower. It sprang free. At the same time, Bill moved the operating lever, pulling the support forward, then reset it.

I was tingling with excitement. The men let out whoops of joy and quickly advanced the rest of the supports. We were now ready to cut the fall area for the second time. We cut and advanced the supports three times during that shift, taking the coalface forward and away from the fall area by a distance of six feet.

My plan had succeeded and the face went on to be an enormous success, producing 1,000 tons a day for the following six months and making almost £500,000. I felt as if I had personally defeated nature by getting past the cavity.

Working in these cavity areas was one of the most dangerous jobs in mining but someone had to do it. At the back of your mind there was the constant fear that if the face stopped production it would lead to the closure of the colliery and that was the last thing that anyone would want.

As you are working in these 'hell holes', humping and heaving railway sleepers and positioning them over the hydraulic chock support, obviously you start to sweat with exertion, but also fear, knowing that at any moment you could be seriously injured or killed.

Several times in my mining career I have missed death or permanent injury by inches, through roof falls or sides collapsing. I often think that someone up there must like me.

In 1968 I was nominated to attend a face management course at Graham House, Benton on the outskirts of Newcastle. Graham House (no relation) was the staff training college of the NCB. The objective of the course was to improve face management to increase face outputs and improve profits.

There were 75 people on the course from all areas of the coalfields including South Wales. Only seven of them, including me, were under-officials. The rest were from senior management level, including managers, deputy managers, under-managers, chief electrical engineers, chief mechanical engineers, unit engineers, and area personnel.

It was a week-long residential course focussing on an exercise in the design, staffing, and organisation of a high production face. We were divided into eight syndicates with a brief to devise a method of producing coal at threepence-halfpenny per therm in a particular seam.

One evening a film was shown of Lord Robens giving a speech on the need to produce coal more cheaply. To me this film was the highlight of the course. It was a real Churchillian-type of speech and when he'd finished, I felt like going straight to the Havannah, there and then, to cut the coalface and start producing coal. Lord Robens was a great motivator; he had such a command of the English language and the knack of being able to communicate with people from all levels in the mining industry. To his credit, it was he who transformed the mining industry from a pick and shovel concern into a highly mechanised business.

The face management course opened my eyes to the enormity of the Coal Board management structure. I never, in my wildest dreams, realised until then how many people were actually employed. And to think, all their wages had to be earned at the pick point! At the time of nationalisation, when the Coal Board took over from the private owners, all the plum jobs in the industry were taken up by the old pit owners, or their descendants, and Hobart House was bursting at the seams with hyphen-Smith-Joneses.

Staying at Graham House was like living in a four star hotel. The night porter would polish your shoes, a maid would wake you up in the morning with a cup of tea, and the food was of the highest quality. Dress was informal but for some occasions a dark lounge suit was desirable. The dining room and lounges were fit for Royalty. There was even a Graham House club; it cost 2s 6d to become an annual member. The Coal Board certainly looked after its staff, particularly its senior management. Apparently there was another college like this one at Chalfont near London.

At first I felt as if I was out of my depth, rubbing shoulders with all these 'big wigs' from the management hierarchy. But as the week progressed I felt more and more confident. After all I was already a 'key' figure in a high productivity unit. Staffing, designing and organising theoretically was, therefore, relatively simple.

At the end of the week's course I returned to normality and the excitement of the coalface. Being on the face management course was like being given a free week's holiday. It had been a completely original experience for me and one that I will never forget. But I think I preferred to get on with the job! It was around this time that television was introduced underground at the Havannah. A camera was placed at the main transfer point near the bottom of the drift, and there was a monitor in the control room at the surface so coals could be seen being loaded onto the cable conveyor. Several years later a second camera was placed at a loading point, approximately half way down the drift where a new development had taken place and was now ready for production. I often wondered what my Dad would have thought about such technology; 20 years earlier he hadn't even seen a television in his own home, let alone down the mine!

Another big improvement underground was the introduction of electric lighting on the coalface and roadways near the face entrance. Obviously it was very costly to install, but it didn't last long on the faces. The lights were continually damaged by shot-firing. There was also the risk of an explosion from the heat of the lighting element if it ever came into contact with methane gas, which was often present underground.

By now, most faces were mechanised. But the two roadways or tunnels, which every face has, were still being worked by conventional methods. That is to say, holes were bored into the strata above the coal seam, they would be charged with explosives and then fired down. Half of the stones from the explosion would then be hand-shovelled onto the conveyor in the roadway and mixed with coals, the other half would be stowed to form packs to support the roadway tunnel.

I had a shot-firer, who was a Grade II deputy, to assist me with the shot-firing operations. All deputies who were not normally required to fire shots always had to carry ten detonators, so that if the shot-firer was required to fire both roadways at the same time (as was often the case), the deputy could fire one of the roadways for him. I remember most vividly one occasion when preparing to fire a tail-gate roadway. I had just stemmed the boreholes with the explosives and placed a couple of sentries at the entrance of the danger zone to prevent anyone from entering the area. I then crawled onto the face for a last inspection, just to make sure that everything was ok, when the spill-plates of the haulage chain whiplashed and struck me hard above the left eye.

For a few seconds I was unconscious, then, after coming round, I put my hand above my left eye and found that it quickly became covered in bright red blood. I shouted to the sentries to come and help me, and they eventually got me off the face and contacted the overman. I was given first aid and then sent immediately to the surface, as my injury required stitches. I was very lucky to get away with just a few stitches, I could have quite easily lost my left eye or even been killed.

I surprised my fellow officials by turning up for work the next day, as most of them thought that I would be off work for at least a couple of weeks. In those days you were financially better off on the sick than you were at work. Being on an upstanding wage when on the sick, you also received sick pay, which was not taxed, and so you ended up being several pounds a week better off. A lot of officials took advantage of this whenever they could, and high absenteeism was quite normal. However, I was so keen to produce coal and make a good name for myself that the thought of staying off work never entered into my head.

Dust became a real problem in the early days of mechanisation. Once coal dust became airborne it was almost impossible to control. It didn't matter how many external sprays were fitted to a machine, they had very little effect on controlling the dust.

If the face encountered a fault, and the machine had to cut through it, the conditions would be so bad that it would be almost impossible to breathe, let alone see in front of you. Men working in the return air tunnels (usually making the tail-gate roadway) would have to stop working and move out of the dusty air stream until the machine had negotiated the fault. Dust masks were provided to cover your nose and mouth, but trying to do anything remotely physical with the masks on was very uncomfortable. It was alright for the officials to wear a mask to walk around the tunnel inspecting the work, but for anyone trying to shovel stones or lug machinery, the conditions were almost inhuman. Improvements were being made and new techniques were being introduced all the time but there was still a long way to go in the battle against dust. The main reason why the men put up with the conditions was the constant fear that the pit would close if production declined.

As a deputy on a high production face, my relationship with the face overman was a very close one. The deputy's job was to carry out the face overman's instructions. The overman's primary responsibility was to ensure that the pit was being run efficiently. He had to see that everything and everyone in his district was performing properly. For example he had to ensure that the deputy carried out his statutory duties; that all the workmen had the correct tools and supplies; that the roadways were kept straight; that the face conveyor alignment and horizon were correct, etc. It was also his job to set priorities and measure progress, and ensure continuity between shifts, as well as give the under-manager as much information as possible, and keep the control room informed of any major delays or breakdowns.

Together with the deputy, the overman was responsible for safety. The overman also co-ordinated the mining, mechanical and electrical operations with the help of the assistant engineers. In modern terms, he was the face manager.

This is the job for me, I thought. And when the next overman's course was announced, I filled in the application form. Not only did I get an interview, I was also one of the 18 men selected for the course. My God I was so proud. By now two of my brothers, Cyril and Reg, were already overmen.

The course was to last 12 weeks, with six weeks at Ashington Technical College, two weeks at the Dame Margaret Hall residential centre, and the other four weeks on visits to other collieries, workshops and mining machinery firms.

We had talks and seminar exercises on cost control, method study, standards of work, communications and the modern approach to management techniques.

I was given a stop-watch and a clipboard, and sent out to several mechanised faces at different collieries to carry out delay studies on various machines. We were also taught how to study work measurement and how to evaluate human work content; the effective deployment of manpower was a big issue. I also visited several collieries and shadowed overmen, following them as they went about their daily duties. I had an insight into the work of the colliery electrical and mechanical engineers and all the various colliery departments.

I really enjoyed the course. Mind you, after all those canteen meals and dinners at home in the evening I had put on a stone in weight.

When I returned to work I was given my old job as deputy on the 1,000 ton a day face. There were no vacancies for overmen at the time. With my head full of newly acquired knowledge and fresh ideas, my main aim was to create a district and face that were so efficient that coal would be produced non-stop. I wanted to eliminate all delays, which is easier said than done and impossible without the co-operation of the workforce. My aim was soon realised, but in the most unusual circumstances.

A fatal accident had occurred in the first shift of the day when a man was killed in a roof fall. Production immediately stopped and the rest of the men from that shift followed the dead man out as he was stretchered to the surface.

When my shift arrived for work all the necessary inspections had been completed and I was told to carry on working as normal but to take extra care because of the weak roof conditions. How on earth could we carry on as normal I wondered with a fellow worker so recently lost. When the men arrived at the meeting station, the place where I would normally test their lamps and issue instructions, not a word was spoken. The men were choked into silence. They went to their work places and set about their jobs without a word. The roadway conveyors that transport the coal to the surface were started up as was the coal cutting and loading machine. Immediately coals started to stream off the face like a black river winding its way along the dark underground tunnels.

A remarkable thing occurred during that shift. The conveyors carrying the coal never stopped once during the entire shift, and neither did the machine cutting the coal, not even during the break for bait. It was the first and only time I could ever remember there being no delays at all. Production from the face never ceased during the whole shift. And during the shift the face was cut almost five times, which was a new record. The men and officials had shown their respect to the dead man in the way they knew best. No one left the face feeling pleased at what they had achieved, just a sense of quiet pride.

In the late 1960s the mechanisation of coal production was in full swing. But because of this, a new stage in the operations had been invented; the removal and transfer of expensive hydraulic supports and cutting machines from a face that had been worked out, on to a new face. The work had to be carried out with as little delay in productivity as possible. At first, everyone thought it was an almost impossible task. To dismantle, transfer and reassemble this kind of machinery in such confined spaces was certainly not easy.

The plan was to take all the hydraulic supports off a 200-yard face, transport them 500 yards along the main roadway, pass them through a small opening, and reassemble them on a new face. It was estimated that all this could be carried out, and that the machines would be ready to operate within 72 hours!

Weeks of planning, right down to the most minute detail, occupied the colliery and area personnel. A control unit was set up at the surface and manned by senior management every hour of the day, right through the weekend. All hydraulic supports were numbered and monitored on two face plans at the surface. The operation was undertaken with military precision and turned out to be a huge success.

Coal production on the old face ceased at 7am on Friday and was restarted at mid-day on the following Wednesday. The new face produced 16 cuts that week. So successful was the operation that it was later used as a role model in senior management training programmes. It illustrated just what could be achieved by area and colliery personnel working together as a team, with the right attitude. I felt very proud to be part of the team during that operation.

In 1970 I was given the chance to prove myself as an overman by the new colliery manager. I was assigned to a face that had encountered a 15 foot fault towards the main roadway end of the face. I realised that it was impossible to negotiate such a thick fault. However, because of the slow angle at which the fault crossed the eventual face line, it was possible to gain a limited amount of coal by bearing the coal right up to the fault.

The manager estimated that we could get at least another 5,000 tons of coal by doing this. Showing me the plan of the district, he asked if I could get him 100 tons of coal per day on a single shift with one team of men. Provided that basic principles and safety standards were followed, I saw no reason why this could not be achieved. At the time the pit was going through a bleak period and every ton of coal produced was vital. Most of the cream had been siphoned off and developments were behind schedule.

I was given a big incentive by the manager in that I could choose any shift that suited me and, provided that I came up with the 'goods', I was to be in sole charge of the operation.

I eventually explained what the manager had asked of me to the men that were under my control. On the whole they were an average set of blokes, except for the four men whose job was to make and advance the tail-end roadway. Those four men were probably the best set of workers in their field, and it was a pleasure to stand and watch the way they tackled their objectives. Each man knew exactly what he had to do and all four men together worked in perfect harmony.

My first priority, before I could allow the face to advance, was to re-establish the stowing area at the tail-end roadway. This is where the stones that had been blasted from the roadway were tightly packed. This operation did two things: it formed the basis of the roadway; and supported the roadway to prevent it from collapsing.

The face had been standing idle for several weeks and the stowing area was completely closed off because the roof had collapsed. There was an area just beyond the stowing area, in the 'goaf', where the roof was still up, unsupported. This was an ideal site for me to re-establish the stowing area, providing that someone brave enough, or stupid enough, would squeeze behind the line of hydraulic supports and erect some wooden supports into the unsupported roof.

Underground, you never ask another man to do something that you would be frightened to do yourself. I explained to the four men what my intentions were and eagerly awaited their reaction. 'You must be a bloody idiot,' said one man 'I wouldn't go in there for a gold pig.' Another said he wouldn't do it for all the tea in China, and the last one said he might consider it if Bridgette Bardot or Marilyn Monroe were lying in there naked, but definitely not if it was just 'wor lass.'

I noticed that the area had already defied all the laws of gravity for several weeks, and by rights it should have collapsed well before now. Perhaps Lady Luck would hold it up just a little longer until I got in and supported it. The men gathered up all the tools I needed. I squeezed myself through the face line supports and got into position behind them so I could build a wood chock support.

The men passed through the wood chocks one by one and eventually I had built a two-foot square solid wood chock from floor to roof. By this time I was really sweating, not from the work I was doing, but out of sheer fright.

No sooner had I finished the first chock when the men said 'OK John, get out of there, that's our work now.' Within minutes those four lads had the area supported and had made it as safe as the Bank of England. After that incident it didn't matter what I asked them to do, if it was humanly possible, they did it. I suppose it's called leading from the front. Perhaps I got this spirit from Mr Rothery, the overman at Prestwick.

Having established the stowing area, my next priority was to cut the face to a plan. I divided the face into sections. It was of paramount importance to keep the face straight and advance the armoured face conveyor (AFC) in one direction. If too much pressure was put onto the AFC it would jack-knife and the whole conveyor was capable of lifting almost to the roof. I had seen this happen before when a technical assistant to the manager (a real whizz kid) was put in charge of a new mechanised unit and he thought he knew it all. As a consequence, the face conveyor ended up jack-knifed and seven days' production were lost!

I often wonder what happened to him.

With only one production shift being worked each day (my shift), I was in complete control of all face operations and I personally supervised the grading alignment and cutting operations. This meant I couldn't blame anyone else if anything went wrong.

The manager's suggestion to swing the face off by the 15 foot fault was a tremendous success and we produced three times the amount of coal first envisaged. The 'face' travelled a further 200 yards and we ended up working on that face for five months.

6 The strikes of 1972 and 1976

By 1972 I was officially appointed as an overman. And by that time we had extracted virtually all the coal from the Prestwick side of the Havannah.

The square mile of coal which was originally to give Prestwick 20 years of life, had been taken out in seven years. Due to mechanisation, production had increased three-fold. What progress!

1972 was also the year of the first national strike since 1926. After years of accepting low wage increases, the miners had eventually had enough and would not stand for the situation any longer. They had already fallen well behind the wage deals in comparable industries.

As I look back and reflect upon how the strike developed, my opinion is that Lord Robens (Chairman of the NCB) had deceived miners for a very long time. Miners were so afraid of the situation of redundancies and pit closures, that up until now they had been afraid to fight for greater wage increases. Because of this situation, miners were now travelling all over the country like 'industrial gypsies'. After all, Lord Robens had closed many more pits in his day, than Mr Magregor had been forced to close under the auspices of Margaret Thatcher.

'A fair day's work for a fair day's pay', was the cry at the time. And we certainly had the right to make such a claim. In 1972, I was earning £32.40 per week; this was £2 a week LESS than I was earning in 1961 on piece-work at Prestwick!

There were four Grahams (including myself) working at the colliery, in three different unions. Cyril and I were members of the National Association of Colliery Overmen, Deputies and Shot firers (NACODS), Reg was a member of the Colliery Officials and Staff Association

(COSAS), and our Ken was a member of the National Union of Mineworkers (NUM). NACODS members worked during the seven-week strike while COSA members, who are affiliated to the NUM, worked part of the first week, but eventually joined the NUM strike.

As a family of four brothers we didn't fall out and call each other blacklegs or scabs, but I certainly felt very guilty in my situation. In effect we were relying on the NUM to secure our next wage rise. For a number of years NACODS had an agreement with the Coal Board officials that whatever increase had been secured for the NUM members, NACODS would maintain a ten per cent increase above their settlement. This naturally infuriated local NUM committee members! As a result of the agreement, all the officials had to do was sit on their backsides and wait until the strike had been resolved.

For seven weeks during the strike, NACODS members kept the conveyors running and the machines ticking over ready for the men to return to work. To alleviate the boredom, some of the officials spent their time making mouse traps and catching mice. Because most of the workers were on strike, there were hardly any scraps of food for the mice and so after a couple of weeks they were becoming desperate and it was very easy to entice them into the traps. I remember one official telling me that after killing a mouse he threw it onto the stationary conveyor belt. Within seconds there were two more mice devouring the dead one. Before long there were no mice at all underground at the Havannah.

One of the jobs I did while at work during the strike was to hew (by hand) coals to take home, as the delivery of concessionary coals had ceased. There was a pillar of coal just around the corner from the overman's office and quite near to the cable belt. Every day I would hew about a hundredweight of coal, put it into a bag and then run it, via the cable belt conveyor, to the surface.

Picketing by the NUM members at the main entrance was friendly and peaceful at first, but as time passed by it became more hostile. At the beginning of the strike I travelled by car to work, stopping at the picket lines to argue with the lads about why I could not support them. My argument was that if they went against the wishes of their union (the NUM), then I would go against the wishes of mine (NACODS). This argument used to infuriate them more and more and they would bang on the roof of the car with their fists and try to rock the car to and fro.

It was eventually decided that all officials would travel to work by bus but on arrival at the colliery they would have to walk through the picket lines. We quickly got used to the jeers and shouts of 'bastard' and 'scab'. On one occasion, as the bus drew up to the colliery, one of the pickets, a man who worked for me in fact, was banging on the window so hard that he smashed his watch and it fell to the ground. At the same time, inside the bus, I was laughing at a joke one of the other officials was telling. However, because of the timing, the picket thought I was laughing at his misfortune, and he never spoke to me again, even after they had returned to work.

Once the strike was over and the men returned to work, most of them had acted as nothing had happened. Some took days before they would talk to officials and others took weeks, but eventually everything got back to normal. Joe Gormley, then the President of the NUM, was quoted as saying 'Settle it over a pint lads,' and this is, in the main, what happened.

People still insist that the 1984 strike would never have lasted as long if Joe Gormley had still been President of the NUM, but I can still remember during the 1972 strike when the general public were calling Joe 'gormless-Gormley'.

During the first shift back to work after the strike, I expected a lot of trouble during production, but quite the opposite happened. We cut the face three times during that shift; well above the normal average.

After being out of production for seven weeks, the effort involved during the first shift back, such as having to crawl up and down the face for most of the shift, was very painful. My wrists and knees were so sore that the usual shower in the pit head baths was not enough to ease the discomfort.

In 1953, when I started working for the Coal Board, there were around 70 collieries working in Northumberland. By 1972 the number had been reduced to 15. The Havannah was now a very cosmopolitan pit with workers drawn from at least 28 pits in Northumberland. I knew in my heart that the day was not very far away when the Havannah, too, would be exhausted. I had already discussed the situation with my wife and we nearly emigrated to Australia, but in the end we decided against it.

In the early 1970s a new tunnelling machine had been introduced to the Havannah. It was known as the Dosco road header and its purpose was to cut, load and tunnel its way through the coal seam and strata at a much faster pace than anything conventional methods could achieve. With the modern mechanised faces moving forward much more quickly due to intensified mining methods, the biggest obstacle to increased production was the development and preparation of the roadways and faces. The Dosco road header removed this obstacle and it was decided the machine would be pushed to its limits; the project was known locally as the 100-yard dash.

The plan was to tunnel 100 yards in a week, through the High Main Seam. Cyril, my eldest brother, was the overman in charge of the operation and it was his responsibility to keep the project running efficiently. He had three teams of three men and each team worked an eight-hour shift, covering 24 hours of the day. Each team had to tunnel eight yards per shift, setting arch girder supports at one-yard intervals. They also had to advance the roadway conveyor belt.

Back-up teams of men laid the supply track on wood sleepers, while another team advanced the conveyor structure. The whole operation was carried out with very high quality workmanship and the first week's results produced an amazing 107 yards of tunnel. In fact, the tunnel was so impressive that photographs were taken of it to commemorate the achievements of the men.

The area deputy director was so confident after the initial stages that he decided to push the men and the machine even further. 'Could a quarter of a mile be achieved in four weeks?' – this was their next target. And, amazingly, after four weeks, 444 yards of tunnelling had been driven. This was a new record.

The makers of the Dosco machine were so pleased with the efforts of the men, and the machine's performance, that they treated all the men involved to a free dinner and 'booze up'. Furthermore, the firm presented each official with a special tie bearing the name of the machine and the numbers 444!

The same type of machine was used in the initial stages of the 1970s Channel Tunnel, until the Government decided to suspend the project.

However, the machine was not without its problems, chief of which was the amount of dust it created. Sometimes the conditions were so bad that you couldn't see your hand in front of your face and often the machine had to be stopped to allow the dust to be sucked up into air bags. But I must also stress that the strata consisted of an extremely hard limestone and I don't know of any other machine that would be capable of cutting through that type of rock.

Now that the face work and roadway preparation were almost totally mechanised, I was always looking for ways in which to improve the efficiency even further. But one of my ideas got me into a lot of trouble.

Most of the electrical switch gear for the face was situated in the tail-gate return roadway and mounted on steel trams. By coupling the train of the electrical switch gear to the armoured face conveyor, every time the face conveyor was rammed forward after each cut the electrical equipment would also advance. I was well pleased with my efforts but I got a real 'bollocking' from the unit electrical engineer for not informing him. Apparently, unknown to me, he had to obtain permission from the inspectorate.

Workers on the face couldn't produce coal effectively without an efficient conveyor system to transport the coal to the surface. It was part of my job to see that this was maintained properly. In the main roads a specialised team of workmen maintained the conveyors and it was very rare for them to break down. On one occasion, though, I remember being the first on the scene when a conveyor belt had broken. Usually, if a belt breaks at all, it breaks at a joint, as this one had. But during my examination of the belt, I found that it had been cut with a sharp instrument almost the whole width of the belt, except for about six inches which had then ripped. It was clearly an act of sabotage.

Not only did the conveyor transport coal to the surface, it was also a man-riding conveyor. If the conveyor had snapped while men were being transported on it, lives could quite possibly have been lost.

After repairing the conveyor, I took the sabotaged joint to the surface to let senior management examine it. The joint was then put on public display at the colliery, to let everyone know that the officials were on the look out for the saboteur. There was not a lot of sabotage at Havannah and generally relations between the men and the officials were quite good. I'm pleased to say that, although the mystery was not solved, no such incident was ever repeated.

February, 1974 signalled the start of the next strike, which involved three-day weeks and power cuts. My union, NACODS, decided at a local meeting that on this occasion it would support the men by not turning up for work. This decision went against the guidelines of our National Executive.

An area member of the Northumberland Executive addressed the meeting at which this decision had been taken, and persuaded the members not to turn up for work by describing what it was like during the 1972 strike at his pit. He said that officials were being intimidated by threats of violence, bricks were being thrown through their windows at home, and striking men's wives were fighting with the wives of the officials in the back lanes while the officials were down the pit. Obviously, they didn't want that situation to arise again, and that is why they had turned up at our meeting.

As far as I knew, the whole of the Northumbrian NACODS union stayed away from work in sympathy with the men. I was on strike for the first, and only, time in my career. With a wife and three small daughters to feed it wa a difficult decision to make. My wife, Ann, had a part-time job and I got £5 a week from the Social Security, but to get it I had to travel 25 miles each week to 'sign on'. I received nothing at all from the union.

The 1974 strike occurred for the same reason as the 1972 strike; increased wages. But this time, at least I could hold my head up and say that I wasn't relying on the NUM to negotiate my wage rise for me while I was still at work receiving full pay. In 1974 Northumberland miners were the only members of NACODS to receive no pay during the strike.

Before, and after, the strike I was put in charge of developing a new 'face' in the two-feet six-inch Brockwell seam. This involved a Dosco machine to do the tunnelling and a team of men blasting out a new 'face' line. Having been used to working in seams that were up to three-and-a-half feet thick, getting used to such low conditions again was torture. In fact, the height of the seam was reduced even further by the presence of the powered roof supports that took up six inches of the already narrow seam. In effect, we were crawling in a seam that was only two feet high!

The length of the face tunnel was over 200 yards long and contained three inherent undulations. These undulations provided a natural pool that collected the water in these workings. These pools of water further reduced our crawling space. In fact, we were so cramped it was impossible to crawl along on our hands and knees; we were forced to snake our way along the tunnel using our elbows.

Because the roof was so low, the positioning of the conveyor and the alignment of the face were of paramount importance. The undulations meant that the smallest amount of deviation would force the cutting machine to cut into the roof or the floor so careful observation and attention to detail were vital throughout the entire process. With undulations, geological faults and a thin coal seam to contend with, dust conditions were terrible. On several occasions the dust was so bad that men working in the tail-gate roadway had to be sent out of the area into a fresh air point.

Trying to control airborne dust underground is almost impossible but many attempts were made to do just that. One method was to place a curtain across the width of the roadway tunnel. Dust was sucked into the curtain by the ventilation fan and became trapped. A water spray would hose down the curtain, washing the dust on to the floor of the roadway where it would find its way into a water channel. It was a crude method but it did have a limited measure of success. Attempts had to be made to control the air in this seam as the air went on to form the air supply for men working in other areas.

On several occasions I have been in the tail-gate roadway when conditions were so bad that not only could you not see, but it was also very difficult to breathe. When this happened I used to bend down on one knee, cover my mouth, close my eyes and hope that the conditions would improve soon.

Working in these conditions, I knew in my heart of hearts that it was only a matter of time before the colliery closed down. The coal was of a very poor quality; it had a high ash content and a low calorific value. We were now scraping the bottom of the barrel in order to maintain productivity. In fact the closure of the Havannah was delayed only because of the manager's attempts. He was originally trained as a surveyor and now tried his utmost to ferret out any seam that could be worked. However the Havannah colliery was set in the middle of a circle and it did not matter in which direction the workings developed, it was now surrounded by exhausted collieries. On top of this there were a lot of geological faults in this area and a portion of the land had been frozen to protect the runway of Newcastle Airport.

I had enjoyed my nine years at Havannah. I had witnessed many changes, work was never dull, and I had experienced nearly every type of mining operation. I had worked on advancing faces, retreat faces, single shearer units, twin shearer units, plough faces, drifts, developments, conventional faces and a trepan shearer. The only thing I had not done was make money. My wages at the Havannah had stood still for almost a decade.

7 Westoe – hope and reality

Sixteen months before the Havannah closed, I successfully applied for a transfer to Westoe colliery at South Shields on the Durham coalfield. It was a coastal Superpit, whose workings stretched six miles from the shaft out underneath the North Sea. The general manager at Westoe had been manager of the Havannah during the late sixties and early seventies, and it was due to his influence that I got a job at Westoe. However, I was prevented from taking a job as overman as the local NACODS union would only allow transferred officials to take jobs at deputy level or below. This was to protect local officials who were in line for promotion. But despite this I continued to receive my overman's rate of pay, protected for two years by the transfer agreement.

The transfer meant that I had to travel a round trip of 60 miles a day. It also meant that my working day lasted for 11 hours from leaving home to returning there after my shift. But I was prepared to accept this situation as I knew that it would be a job for life. The only other alternative would have meant moving to the Midlands, something I was not prepared to do.

I was given my last day off at the Havannah so that I could go over to Westoe and sign on for work. I was met by the union secretary and during my conversation with him we were interrupted by the general manager who showed us both into his office. I was given a cup of tea while the manager showed me a plan of the workings in the district where I would be placed. 'You have now become a hillbilly' the manager informed me. 'What the bloody hell's a hillbilly?' I asked. 'All transferred men from the collieries are referred to as hillbillies or travellers and the hillbillies refer to the Westoe locals as Sandys or Sand Dancers,' said the manager, laughing. 'It's just the local custom.'

'I am expecting good results from John,' the manager said to the union secretary. 'He is a go-getter and I could do with a few more like him.' 'He will need to be,' said the union secretary, 'to motivate the militant bloody idiots we have here.' Going through my mind was, 'What the hell have I let myself in for? I've moved to a strange pit in a strange area with 2,000 men and only the general manager known to me!' But at least I had the satisfaction that he was on my side; he wanted coal and I wanted to produce it. All my working life I got on very well with my colliery managers mainly because of my pioneering attitude; the coal's down there – go and get it, as safely and economically as possible.

Knowing the general manager wasn't really an advantage. After leaving his office I was introduced to my new union chairman and then taken to the personnel manager's department to sign on. I'd never worked in a pit with a personnel department! At Prestwick and Havannah, all we had was the manager's clerk to deal with all our problems. At Westoe, not only was there a personnel manager but he also had an assistant and a clerk.

My cup of tea with the general manager made me half an hour late for my appointment with the personnel manager, and this had obviously upset him as he was very curt and officious with me. I thought he could have been more helpful as I was a complete stranger in a totally new area. I was in and out of his office in ten minutes. 'Good day, any problems let me know.' He stood up, offered me his hand and that was that. 'He's got a good job,' I thought to myself, 'I wonder what he does?'

I was then introduced to the training officer who took me on a guided tour of the baths, the lockers, the lamp room and the heapstead. The baths, compared to those at my former collieries, were disappointing: they were obviously much larger and contained showers both upstairs and downstairs, but there was a stale foisty smell and attention to hygiene was distinctly lacking. A lick of paint wouldn't have been overdue.

On the heapstead I stood and watched the cage as it ascended to the surface. I could hardly believe my eyes. Up came this huge steel box with three separate decks, each holding 50 men. 150 men travelled up the shaft at any one time. I was completely stunned. At Prestwick, only four men could travel in the cage at a time – that was merely a toy compared to this.

The cage descended to three levels – one at 623 feet, one at 923 feet, and another at 1,300 feet. The middle level was the one most often used. The lower level had no workings, just a return airway to the other shaft (which was known as the crown shaft). The upper level had a limited production life.

That day I was also supposed to meet my new under-manager but owing to a derailment underground no one knew what time he would eventually get to the surface. Instead, I met him the following Monday at ten o'clock, when I started my first day's work at Westoe.

To get to work I travelled ten miles by car and 20 miles by private coach, leaving my car at the first pick-up point, a pub car park. (Four years later I would travel all the way by car).

After a 55 minute journey the bus arrived at the colliery at leaving me 20 minutes to get changed and collect my lamps, identity discs and self-rescuer. I reported to the colliery overman, as instructed and he took me onto the heapstead ready to go underground.

Getting into the cage was an experience in itself. There was a lot of pushing and shoving, and a complete lack of discipline. Men who got into the cage first seemed very reluctant to move to the back of the cage, making it very difficult for the last few men to get in. To me it seemed like sheer stupidity, but it appeared to be the accepted practice.

All three decks of the cage were loaded at the same time and it took a good five minutes to get everyone in. It's here that the jokes start flying around. One man said to the banksman just before the cage started to descend, 'Hey lad, if I wor as ugly as you, I wouldn't know which end to put me false teeth in.' Another man shouted, 'He's that ugly, the wife keeps his photograph on the mantle-piece to keep the bairns away from the fire.'

In the cage you were squashed in like sardines. And someone always broke wind (probably due to nerves), and the smell was disgusting. Slowly, at first, the cage lowered, but then quickly gathered speed until it seemed as if you were dropping like a stone. Your feet seemed to be pushing against your knees and the cage was filled with air rushing about in all directions, so quickly that unless you closed your eyes they really stung.

After a minute or so the cage started to slow down, always over-shooting the light shining in from the inset. Gradually the cage was lifted back up to the correct level and all three decks were emptied. The middle deck was at seam level and there were stairs for use by the men on the upper and lower decks.

The enormity of the shaft area took my breath away. White-washed walls supported large girders, standing to attention like tin soldiers. The noise of the cage closing behind me was deafening, hissing and clanking as the doors slid along on runners powered by compressed air rams.

About 20 yards from the cage you turned off to the right into a brightly lit, white-washed, arched tunnel. Two small, battery-operated locomotives, each with their own train of carriages, waited patiently to take you off to the coalface workings about four miles away from the shaft, under the North Sea. The journey took about 30 minutes. Each locomotive set was capable of carrying 180 men at 12 miles an hour. A single carriage was divided into four compartments with six men in each. The carriages were identical to the ones used at the Havannah.

Sitting on hard wooden benches, with three men to a bench and travelling in complete darkness is not the most comfortable way to start work. Some men managed to nod off, while others might have a game of cards but this tended to be frowned on by the management – silly really because they would be more alert at the end of the journey than those who had fallen asleep.

Each train had its own guard who sat in the last carriage beside the emergency brake, and signalled to the driver, by means of a whistle, when he was ready to move off. Traffic lights were placed at various points along the tunnel to control the movement of man-riding trains and trains carrying supplies. Curtains hung across the carriage entrance to help keep the cold out, but despite these, travelling along the main roadways in winter was a chilling experience.

The journey ended at the 'inbye' locomotive station, a long, arched, white-washed tunnel with two tracks running parallel for 200 yards and points and crossings at each end to allow the loco to change ends ready for the next journey.

At the far end of the station is the colliery overman's office, which also served as the underground deployment point for that district. From here men who did not have a regular workplace were given a job, and men who were absent from work were replaced by others. The colliery overman then deployed the officials to their various districts. After the officials and workmen had been sent to their various districts, the control centre at the surface was told which districts were being worked, and where men were placed.

After a cup of tea and a snack, which lasted about ten minutes, I was taken further towards the coalface workings. I first noticed how dry the roadway was – I expected the conditions to be much wetter than they were – after all, we were underneath the North Sea. Eventually I did experience very wet conditions but in a different seam that was 300 feet nearer the sea bed.

I had a further half-hour journey ahead of me via two man-riding conveyors before we eventually got to the face. We were now 900 feet below the sea bed and four and half miles away from the shaft.

As we journeyed towards the face the overman explained to me that the colliery was really four pits in one. There were four separate underground districts, each with their own underground manager who had statutory responsibility for their district. There was also a fifth under-manager who was responsible for the main roads leading to the shaft as well as the two main underground shafts; he was known as the service manager. Above the under-manager was the deputy manager; he assisted the general manager in formulating the colliery's operational plan. He ensured that all the day-to-day operations underground fulfilled the operational plans, and that they were carried out in accordance with statutory requirements, NCB directives and the manager's rules. He also deputised for the general manager in his absence. Both he and the general manager had a heavy responsibility for over 2,000 men working in seven different shifts producing over one million tons of coal each year.

A 15-minute ride on the conveyor brought us to the tail-gate roadway entrance to the face. We were now in the Brass Thill seam which is around six feet thick! It was unbelievable for me to view a seam that thick after having been used to working in seams less than a third of that height.

Arriving at the face after a 400-yard walk up to the tail-gate roadway, I found myself at one of the most modern coalfaces in Britain. The roadway was supported by steel arch girders and packs of manufactured stone. They looked like chalk, reinforced with wire mesh.

But despite being in this thoroughly modern mine, I couldn't believe what was happening. Stones that had been blasted from above the coal seam, which usually formed the basis of the roadway entrance on to the face, were being hand-shovelled on to the conveyor, mixed with the coals, and sent to the surface while manufactured stones were transported from the surface to the coalface and stowed in place of the natural stones! It was just plain crazy, and the cost must have been astronomical.

The overman took me across the face to the main-gate roadway. I marvelled at the conditions, the tunnels were almost six feet high with large hydraulic roof supports. There were two cutting-loading machines with cutting discs that moved up and down with the touch of a button. Fundamentally, it was no different to what I had been used to, except that the scale was now immense.

It was strange to see men working on the face with their clothes on as I had been used to men working semi-naked. Very few men wore knee pads except for those making the roadways. When both cutting machines were in operation, watching the coals run off the face onto a conveyor was a sight to behold; a stream of large and small coals winding their way along the roadway tunnel and disappearing out of sight into the darkness.

Four men were preparing to advance the main-gate roadway roadway. The roadway was so high (12 feet) that the work had to be done with the aid of scaffolding – long wooden battens stretching along the full width of the place and supported by straight girders that were attached to the arch girders. The scaffolding was about five feet high and the men stood on it in order to bore holes into the stone lip above the coal seam. The lip was then fired down onto the chain conveyor and most of the stones were mixed with the coals and sent to the surface. The rest of the stones were stowed inside a wooden box behind the legs of the arch girders, forming a tight pack between the roadway and the waste area that prevented the roadway from collapsing.

When the stones had been fired down, a large cavity was created in the space. This was supported by large girders. Each girder was formed by fitting together a crown piece and two legs. The crown is the first part of the arch girder to be set, then the two legs are positioned to form an elongated semi-circle. The girders were attached together using steel struts. This is how the roadway tunnel is formed.

After having travelled around the whole of the production district, the overman took me to see the machine that was developing the next coalface unit. This was taking place right next door to the current production unit. The machine was designed to make roadways but only in the coal seam itself (it was not designed to cut stone) and was known locally as 'the miner.' It cut a road into the seam, usually fourteen feet wide and six feet high.

Next I was taken to see the staple, an underground shaft between two seams. Its main function was to provide storage space, but it also replaced the main shaft during a temporary stoppage. Staples could store various amounts of coal, depending on their dimensions; this particular shaft could store around 500 tons of coal.

I realised that there was no difference in the mining operations between Westoe and the other collieries I had been used to working in, except that everything at Westoe was so much bigger. Being able to walk down the face instead of having to crawl was the biggest difference.

My next two shifts were spent with the colliery overman, visiting different working places and generally getting to know the district and fellow officials.

In the next few weeks I was assigned to a shot firing job. I was sent to the tail-gate roadway to blast down the stones for the men after they had bored the holes. This was the same tail-gate roadway that I had visited on my first day at work. Having to do this job again, I felt as if I had been downgraded.

After a couple of shifts I decided that the men were lazy, inefficient, and their general attitude to work was that they couldn't care less. They certainly had no intention of working at a pace I was familiar with. However, in the following week I was still in the same shift but with a different team of men, and their attitude to the job was completely the opposite. They were organised, cheerful, very efficient and nothing upset them. In the third week I was working with a different set of men again, as the face was producing on a three shift, three week cycle. They were humorous and likeable lads, but they couldn't care less whether the work got done or not.

The face was managed very badly, there was no overall plan of production, each shift got what they could and 'bugger everyone else'! Instead of the face and roadways advancing as one single unit, the face progressed quickly but the roadways were not being supported (or constructed) at the same pace. This caused roadways to collapse and close so the face had to stand, without being cut, while the roadways caught up. It would have been much safer and more productive to allow the roadway to dictate the advance of the face. But no one seemed to care about this; it was simply a case of bad planning and poor management by all concerned.

There were no daily or shift measurements of coal advance taken by the officials. Only weekly measurements by the colliery overman were recorded. 'How do you keep the face line straight,' I enquired. 'If you don't use the tape measure?' 'Use your bloody eyes,' I was told.

One of the chief reasons why the roadways were not advanced as quickly as they should have been was that the men were loath to use a shovel. Some of the older men, who were used to conventional methods including using shovels, could manage the work quite easily. It was the younger men that were reluctant to do it. The colliery had the machines to eliminate conventional tunnel construction but the face design was not organised to accept it.

At this particular time, one of the roadway makers was also an NUM committee member who, twice a week on the day shift, would prepare for work, travel underground and, after reaching the coalface, immediately turn around and go back to the surface to attend the consultative meeting as the NUM representative. I then had to record his shift in the time book as normal so that he could receive his pay. When I questioned this practice I was told by my fellow officials that it was the accepted thing to do and it was in agreement with the senior management. I just shook my head in bewilderment at the pure waste of time and money.

At Westoe there were now six production faces, twenty or more development machines and a daily target of 6,000 tons. I knew from experience at my two other collieries that the potential was there for one face to produce the whole of the colliery's present output given the right planning, management and attitude. But, as all unions were hostile to redundancies, they weren't keen on improvements in efficiency that might cost jobs.

Eventually the pace of the roadway development was so far behind the development of the face workings that plans had to be drastically altered. A mechanical shovel was brought in to speed up the work. It was a small, electrically operated tractor mounted on caterpillar tracks with a large hydraulic shovel on the front. This machine had some degree of success and the mechanical shovel was maintained, but it did not provide the answer. So production on this face was still limited to the pace at which the roadway advanced.

There were two machines on the face for cutting and loading the coals. Both were equipped with ranging arms which meant that they could raise and lower their cutting discs by means of a hydraulic ram. They were probably the most advanced cutting and loading machines of their time. I was told by one of the officials that the same type of machine had been used in another part of the mine not only to cut the face, but also to profile the tail-gate roadway. This meant that by raising the cutting disc above the seam it could cut out sufficient stone to form the roadways and thus eliminate the boring and blasting processes. It also did away with the tedious and monotonous job of shovelling up the stones, as they were automatically dropped onto the conveyor.

'Why don't we do it here?' I enquired. I was told that it had not been a success as it took too much time to cut, timber and support the roof, and so delayed production. And so things were just left the way they were.

There was an abundance of overtime to be worked at Westoe, the officials almost guaranteed six shifts a week! I could hardly believe my eyes on the first weekend shift that I worked. It was 6am on a Saturday and there were around 400 men on the heapstead waiting to go underground. 'Where on earth could they all be going?' I thought to myself. Production was not allowed to take place at weekends. The only work carried out was general maintenance, safety checks, repairs and the advancement of a roadway if it was behind schedule.

The working conditions, dust-wise, were terrible at times. Even if you did wear a mask, it soon became impossible to shovel stones at the same time. Every few minutes the men would down tools and out came the snuff boxes. Westoe was notorious for the number of men who took snuff; nearly everyone did from the new entrants right up to the deputy manager. I nearly became addicted but gave it up before that happened.

After my first three months at Westoe I was beginning to wish that I had never laid eyes on the place. A lot of the officials thought that I was a spy for the general manager, the workmen were much more militant than any I had known before and the efficiency of the operations left a lot to be desired. How could it be that miners on the Durham side of the Tyne appeared to be much more militant and argumentative than those on the Northumberland side? Some people say that it goes back to the days of private ownership when the owners of the Durham pits treated the workers like animals, while the Northumberland owners generally looked after their mining communities more humanely (although this was not true in my Dad's case).

I thought I had worked all the shift times possible until I came to Westoe. By the end of my career I must have started or finished a shift in every hour of the 24-hour clock. At Prestwick as a cutter operator, I had worked every conceivable shift to suit the face and to benefit the colliery. Some of the shifts were very unusual, but at least we only worked them during emergencies. For a limited period I worked what was known as a split shift which meant I started half way through the regular shift and finished half way through the following shift. These hours were, on the whole, better than the main shift.

Being such a large colliery, Westoe worked seven different shifts and, for people like me who lived 20 or 30 miles away from the colliery, some of the times were inhuman. For instance, for one shift I had to get out of bed at 2am, for another it would be 4am, and another 6am. On some shifts I would have to leave the house at 10am, 12.30 pm, 3 pm, or 8.30 pm. Some of the finishing times were also very awkward. After one shift

I used to get home at 1.30 in the morning, another at 5.45 in the morning. It got so bad that at times I didn't know whether I was coming or going. Try to imagine getting out of bed at 2am, or going out to work at 8.30pm on a Friday, when your friends are just going dancing or out to the pub.

In my 34 years of mining I had only lost two voluntary shifts from work for reasons other than sickness or injury. Not a bad record.

One of my problems when travelling a round journey of 60 miles to work was trying to stay awake on my way home. After some shifts I used to get so tired after I'd been travelling for about 20 minutes (it usually took me 40 minutes to get home), that I had to pull into a lay-by and get out of the car for some fresh air to waken myself up. On one occasion I actually nodded off at the wheel and ran off the road. Another time I ended up in a field, having ploughed through a three-feet-wide, three-feet-deep ditch, breaking off one of the back wheels and dismantling a gate post. On another occasion I was brought to my senses by the sound of a car horn. Looking up, I found myself in the middle of the road with a car coming straight towards me. We both managed to swerve out of the way at the very last minute, missing one another by inches. One winter, the road conditions were so bad due to snow that I arrived home five hours later than my normal time. On several occasions I have had to take rest days, or days off in lieu, because of these poor travelling conditions.

Although I felt down in the dumps during the first few months at my new colliery, my financial position improved dramatically. Not only were miners back on top of the wages league for industrial workers, but I was also guaranteed an extra shift every week if I wanted to, which increased my wage packet by 20%. At my previous colliery, overtime for overmen was rostered so that you got to work an extra shift every six or seven weeks. My new financial position was so good that from June 1975 through to October 1976 I was able to save almost £2,000 for a deposit on a house, becoming a home owner for the very first time.

There is a saying about work that 'money sweetens the labour', and it was certainly true in my case. However, within a few months everything improved, and I was accepted by the workmen and my fellow officials. Mining folk in all communities tend to be suspicious of any stranger, whether miner or otherwise.

When I worked overtime at weekends I was quite often sent to other parts of the mine. This enabled me to get a much broader picture of the size of the underground workings at Westoe, and would also be useful in the event of an emergency. I was told by an assistant surveyor that around 27 miles of roadway had been driven at Westoe in the construction of developments, production districts and drifts. Travelling around the districts I was able to see why Westoe was thought of as being four collieries in one. It was so enormous that it was physically impossible to travel around the whole of the colliery in a day, never mind in one shift.

In 1975, on the face I had first visited when starting at Westoe, we met what I thought was a fault. The coal had disappeared, leaving a wall of stone where the coal seam should have been. Normally, when encountering a fault, you are usually given some indication as to which way the coal seam has gone, either up or down. However, on this occasion, after extensive boring and drilling we still could not find the coal. Eventually, scientists and geologists came to the conclusion that a pre-historic river must have washed away the coal seam millions of years ago. This unexpected occurrence put back the development of the district by at least two years.

The public were constantly being told that modern mining was much safer than it was in Victorian times, and new coalfaces with modern technology were becoming almost like factories. To a certain degree this was true, but in the case of Westoe, working underneath the North Sea was an additional hazard. I was told in 1974, just after the strike, that there was a rush of water into the underground workings in the 5/4 seam, flooding the district.

The water rushed in so quickly that the pumping system could not cope with it. Larger pumps and pipe ranges were rushed in from all over the country and men were asked to work as much overtime as they could in order to control the floods; some men worked shifts of 24 hours. Eventually the inrush was controlled and, luckily, no lives were lost. The obvious question to be asked was, where did the water come from?

After analysing the water, scientists discovered that it contained seven times the amount of salt contained in normal sea water. This led them to conclude that it was not the sea that had flooded into the district but an underground lake beneath the sea bed. What worried me was the possibility that we might encounter another underground reservoir but not be so lucky the next time.

Although no lives were lost, the machine, conveyors and electrical equipment could not be salvaged, and the area had to be sealed off. An official who had witnessed the incident told me he'd seen nothing like it in all his years of mining.

In November 1976 I was transferred to the 5/4 seam, quite near where the inrush had occurred. At first it was an awful damp, dull and dim place with water constantly seeping in through the roof, making conditions wet and miserable. Ironically, a dry sense of humour existed amongst the officials working that seam and they were constantly making remarks as to how they came to be there. One man said he came on a visit several years ago and had remained there ever since, another said he only came to deliver a message, whilst a third one said he was looking for a shovel and had got lost.

I could see that the area had an enormous amount of potential with vast reserves still to be exploited. In fact, this district was eventually to become the life blood of the colliery. The most immediate problem was flooding. As the workings were only 600 feet below the sea bed, large quantities of water had to be pumped up to the surface. Two large reservoirs, capable of holding millions of gallons of water, had been made on the low side of the district and all water seeping through the roof and seam was channelled into them.

I was put in charge of a production shift on the new, highly-mechanised twin-shearer loader on a 250-yard-long advancing face. It was equipped with very modern self-advancing roof supports and the coal was conveyed from the face with two 200HP electrical motors driving the armoured flexible face chain conveyor.

The face chain conveyor loaded and transferred the coal from the face on to a short chain conveyor in the main roadway, known as the stage loader (which also houses all the controls, telephones and display units that monitor lock-outs of the face). It delivered coals onto the main-gate conveyor belt and eventually on to a main trunk belt. Three trunk belts and two miles later, the coals were poured into a staple acting as a storage bunker. From the staple it was delivered onto another trunk belt system and into a second staple. Then it was put onto the main shaft belt conveyor, and eventually into the shaft skip winder and sent to the surface, travelling a total of five miles.

I was shown around my district which comprised two parallel roadways separated by the 250-yard face. I was introduced to the men as their new deputy, and to the shot-firer who was to assist me. The first thing he told me was that he had no experience of mechanised production faces as he usually worked on the development drivages. He didn't know any of the workmen, he was in the wrong shift, and he had only been sent to this district to assist me for the day. 'Just leave the statutory duties and the running of the district to me. You fire the ripping lips when needed,' I told him.

Here I was at a superpit, five miles from the shaft, 600 feet under the North Sea bed, with a modern, fully equipped face, then worth in excess of £1,000,000, and my only assistant was an official who was not familiar with production. I was in sole charge. This meant that I was responsible for production, the efficiency of the shift (including the transportation of supplies to the face, and the conveying of coals to the surface), as well as the safety of all the men. I was certainly thrown in at the deep end!

Over the next few days I gradually got to know my fellow officials and workmen, but it wasn't easy as it involved over 100 men. I worked a four-shift cycle, with coal being produced in three shifts. No coal was produced in the ten o'clock shift because the face workers wouldn't work that shift. A skeleton team of volunteers carried out maintenance and preparation during this shift.

It took me three months to cover all the shifts and work with all the men. Getting to know them all personally was a hard task. I thought the workers in my previous district had been militant but they were angels compared with this lot. The attitude of most of them to their job, the officials, and management was a disgrace. They didn't care whether coal was produced or not and apathy was everywhere.

It wasn't confined to just one particular shift either, but to all shifts. No matter who was asked a question, the reply was always 'I don't know', and whenever you asked a man to do something he would nearly always tell you that it wasn't his job, or this wasn't right or that wasn't right. If you gave a man a job to do at the beginning of his shift, he thought that that was the only job he had to do during the whole shift. 'One man one job', was their motto. Quite often you were simply told to eff off.

A typical example of a normal shift inspection as a deputy begins at the kist. After I had told all the men where they would be working, I would phone through to control at the surface and tell them which places were being worked and how many men were sited there. I would then have a quick snack and a browse through the reports of the previous 24 hours before beginning my inspection.

Normally an official started his inspection at the main road entrance with an examination of the conveyor drive unit, checking the belt alignment, making sure that the unit wasn't overheating and testing for the presence of gas. Much of this work was repetitive and quite boring but vital to safety, and you had to be methodical in your approach as you quite often got distracted from your work if there was an emergency, or an injury, or if supplies were not available, or if production had stopped because the men were being uncooperative.

Usually the first workmen you would encounter on your way to the face were the supply lads. These were teenagers waiting their turn for coalface training. They always greeted you with the same three questions: one, can they have more pay than stipulated for the job?; two, can they have an excessive wet payment (for working in wet conditions)?; and three, is there any chance of a sharp 'lowse'? (an early ride before the end of the shift).

Quite often, during an emergency for example, a small part of machinery might have to go to the surface for welding. This is when you would send a couple of the supply lads to the surface with the part to check that it was being repaired, and to make arrangements for it to be returned underground. However, more often than not, this system was abused and lads were given fictitious jobs or sent up when it wasn't necessary.

As to the system of excessive wet notes, it was regularly abused. Most officials used this wet note as an inducement to get work done, it acted as a sort of bribe! The Deputies also used this payment to show favouritism, for example, if he didn't like a particular workman and, at the end of the shift, he wasn't particularly wet then he wouldn't get a wet note. If he did like him but he wasn't wet, he would get a wet note.

The excessive wet agreement was so vague that you could drive a steam roller through it. But, if common sense prevailed it was sometimes adhered to. Periodically, pressure from senior management forced officials to tighten up on the issue of the notes as, in some cases, workers had been discovered to sign their own wet notes! When the tightening up occurred, co-operation between the workmen and officials deteriorated and after a couple of weeks bribery began to creep back in.

On one occasion, I was told by senior management to pay a greater rate of pay for the job of getting the supplies to the face to compensate the lads for their loss of wet notes. Such practices were alien to me and I just shook my head in disbelief. Eventually, after the 1984 strike the deputy manager vetted all wet notes and if he deemed a district was not excessively wet no payments were made.

To pacify the supply lads, after answering no to all their questions, I would try a little psychology. If, in the event of an emergency, a certain item had to be sent to the surface for repair, I promised them that they would be the first to be considered as they were my favourites. I used this same method on the lads in the tail-gate roadway as well! It was amazing the number of times a mechanised production unit relied on the whims of these young lads to keep production going.

The faceworkers (who thought that they were the elite of mining) adamantly refused to carry equipment, even in an emergency. Their attitude was that the 'face' could stand for as long as it took, and the longer the better.

I remember on one occasion persuading a machine operator to carry a vital part of equipment underground. The part was so important that without it production could not continue. (Each district did have its supply of spare parts, but it was impossible to keep a stock of all parts as the cost would have been tremendous). One of the face workers found out that the machine operator was carrying a small part and started to mock him; the rest of the workers joined in until embarrassment forced the man to leave the part on the heapstead. However, he didn't tell me so there was a further delay of two hours once we had reached the face while I sent one of the lads back to the heapstead to get the part.

This practice of non co-operation was rife throughout the colliery. Fitters and electricians tended to be the same way inclined and often the assistant engineers ended up being loaded down like pack mules because the other workers refused to help out. It was usually left to the officials and engineers to do the donkey work.

I felt sorry for the young supply lads because coalface training was ceasing and there were no jobs available for the lads who had finished their training either: the training system was beginning to stagnate.

Leaving the supply lads to get on with their jobs, I would carry on examining the roadway leading to the face, as well as giving the conveyor belt and its support structure a visual examination. The next person I met would be the stage loader attendant. His job was to operate the stage loader conveyor and the face chain conveyor. It is a simple job and requires very little physical effort as both conveyors were mechanically operated by the push of a button. The stage loader has several functions: it acts as a short scraper chain which allows the heading machine to advance approximately 30 yards in front of the face, it is attached at right angles to the AFC chain and transferred coal from the face on to the main road trunk belt, 70% of the stones from the ripping lip were hand-filled on to the stage loader chain, and, in addition to all of this, all the electrical equipment for the face and advance heading, plus telephones and display units that monitor lockouts on the face are all mounted and carried on the stage-loader. It also housed the First Aid equipment and a morphine safe.

The stage loader attendant (usually a young trainee) was responsible for keeping the 'black stream' of coals in motion as they are transferred from the stage loader on to the central trunk belt, and so minimise spillage. This is a lot easier said than done and a young attendant who is good at his job is a boon to the official of the district. Being able to adjust the belt rollers to suit the load depends on experience and common sense. If, for example the night shift did not keep the stage loader in line when advancing it, a lot of work was created for the attendant in cleaning up the spillage. Quite often I would find the attendant steaming with sweat as he attempted to hand fill the spillage from the top belt on to the bottom belt, consequently choking the return drum. Inevitably the belt would break and production would be stopped.

I remember on one occasion arriving at the stage loader to find the poor attendant stripped to the waist, shovelling spillage for all he was worth in an attempt to keep production going, while ten yards away four men were sitting on their backsides telling jokes and acting as if they didn't have a care in the world. 'Come over here and give a hand,' I shouted at them. 'What for?' came the reply. 'It'll only take us ten minutes to clean up the spillage and get production going again.' By now the face conveyor had been locked off and the machine was standing.

'It's not our effing job,' someone replied. 'Get them lazy bastards off the face to clean up.' I walked down to where they were sitting, grabbed the first one I came to by the neck and lifted him up. 'What did you say lad?' I screamed at him. 'Are you refusing an instruction?' I acted as if I had gone completely mad. The workman got such a fright, he grabbed hold of the shovel I had been using and started to clear up some of the spillage. His other three mates did likewise.

One of them mumbled 'I'll see the union about you.' 'You can shove the union up your backside,' I replied. 'You're not coming into my district and refusing instructions. You do as I say, not what your union says.' I hated workmen who thought they could frighten me by threatening me with the union. I had no time at all for them and thought they lacked character and didn't have the guts to stand up for themselves.

Having cleaned up the spillage and adjusted the conveyor alignment, we were in a position to start up production again. The four men started to walk away, 'Where the bloody hell do you think you're going?' I asked. 'We've got to load up a damaged machine part for the surface. The colliery overman has sent us in to get it.' 'OK,' I said 'But before you do there's eight complete arches to unload and advance up to the road head for the stoneman. You can give a hand to the supply lads and then you can go and load your part.' As I walked away I heard one of them say 'That bastard likes his pound of flesh doesn't he!'

I always took great care to see that there was no spillage at the stage loader before moving on to my next inspection which was the ripping lip. Four men would be preparing to advance it by boring holes into the lip and blasting it down with explosives. Their usual complaint was that the men in the previous shift had not done their job properly, supports were missing, there was not enough lagging available to do the job, this was not right, that was not right.

According to them, no more arch-girder supports had been set in since they'd set the last one. They felt that they were the only shift doing any work on the advancement of the roadway. After making sure that they had all the necessary equipment and supplies I would move on to the face and into the advance heading.

The advance heading forms the front of the main-gate roadway roadway. The coal is extracted about 30 yards in front of the face, forming a hollow chamber. This area has to be ventilated by an auxiliary fan which is carried and mounted by the stage loader. Ventilation air bags from the fan are stretched along the stage loader, passed underneath the ripping lip and eventually right up the face of the heading.

Every time the ripping lip is fired down, or dropped (local term) the men have to come out from the heading as the ventilation bags have to be parted and put out of the way of danger until the shot-firing of the ripping lip is completed. Once the firing of the lip is completed it has to be dressed and squared off. This is done on the newly-erected scaffolding by a man using a long, iron pinch bar. He pokes and levers down loose stones, preparing the area ready for the setting of the crown piece of the next supporting arch, and so advancing the tunnel.

It was while this was happening that chaos sometimes broke out. The man on the scaffolding refused to allow the heading men to re-couple the ventilation bags until he had squared up the ripping lip, he also refused to work with the stage loader chain running, claiming that the noise distracted him! And so production had to be stopped.

Once the man on the scaffold had given the OK, the heading men started to re-couple the air bags. However, to do this they stood on the stage loader scraper chain, which meant that production still stood as the scraper chain had to be locked off. It was a very bad system, which could be altered only through better attitudes. The awkward worker who liked to delay production had a field day during this operation.

Arguments raged between the stonemen and the heading men as to whose job it was to re-couple the air bags. Eventually, after losing about 30 minutes of production, work resumed. The heading men could, if they were in the mood, advance the heading machine forward by at least fifteen to eighteen feet and set five or six girders in one shift. But because of their attitude they often managed to set only one or two, and were forever blaming the machine for breaking down.

The next part of my inspection involved two men working at the immediate entrance to the face. One of their jobs was to advance two girders running parallel to each other in front of the ripping lip. They also had to advance and ram over the drive unit and build a wood chock parallel to the road tunnel and the edge of the waste area. It was a good job to have, as the amount of work they had to do depended on how many times the face was cut in that shift. On average they only worked about one fifth of their shift.

Continuing on my inspection, the next men I encountered were the machine operators and the chockmen. The machine men cut the face and the chockmen rammed the face conveyor forward into the new track and then advanced the hydraulic roof supports (the chocks). These men were the core workers of the coal industry, the men who produce the coal and were the highest paid.

Due to the face design on this particular face, two machines were used to cut the coal. One machine was the main-gate machine, the other the tail-gate machine. Both were electrically powered and both were hauled along the face using the same steel-linked haulage chain. The main-gate machine cut two-thirds of the face and the tail-gate machine cut the other third. Both machines were similar in design except that one was a right hand machine and the other was a left hand machine.

They cut and loaded most of the coals from the top section of the seam, and then cut out the bottom section on the return journey. To complete one strip of coal two feet deep and six-and-a-half feet high, both machines cut out until they met together, then with the use of hydraulic rams built into the gearhead, the cutting discs were lowered so that they could core away at the bottom section of the seam.

By the time the machines started on the return journey, the plough run, a gap of two feet had been created between the AFC and the face. The roof had also been exposed by two feet from the edge of the cantilever support up to the face.

The AFC was then pushed forward two feet using horizontal hydraulic rams built in to each hydraulic support. These rams have a dual purpose, as well as pushing the AFC forward, they also allowed each hydraulic support, when lowered, to pull themselves forward two feet and into the new position. The cantilevers were then raised by other hydraulic rams and set tight to the roof once again. The roof behind the supports was allowed to collapse and it caved in under its own weight. It was a simple, straightforward job. Although underground work in the UK coal industry in modern times was exclusively carried out by men, in America women are often employed as machine operators. The job is quite boring and repetitive in normal conditions but when conditions are bad it becomes the most dangerous job in modern day mining.

Roof falls caused cavities of varying sizes. They had to be secured, usually by constructing a wood trellis on top of the cantilever supports. Sometimes the cavities were so enormous that it was impossible to support the roof so we had to construct a false roof using battens that were similar to railway sleepers.

If the cavity was anything up to six feet above the cantilever the men were able to build on top of the supports and choke the area with timber. Conditions such as these were very dangerous as someone had to get on top of the support to build the trellis without anything supporting them!

Building a trellis meant that at any time the loose, unsupported strata could fall on top of you. At times, conditions have been so bad that workmen refuse to do the job and then it falls to the officials, or those that are prepared to do it. I am often asked why I would risk my life for the sake of the Coal Board, but someone had to do it, and afterwards I would be filled with a tremendous sense of satisfaction. I have defied nature, done the impossible and been where no other man would go. In return I've earned the respect of senior management, the men and my fellow officials.

Often there was no indication as to whether the powered roof support was working or not; sometimes the supports would lower off for no apparent reason (although it was usually due to faulty ball bearings in the hydraulic system). Later models had pressure gauges fitted indicating what pressure was being put on to each leg of the support, so at least I knew that the support was working.

It was while working in terrible conditions like this I often wondered what the general public would have thought had they been able to see inside the mine.

It was a difficult task to complete and much thought had to be put into how to approach it. You had to examine the situation very carefully. What was the extent of the fall area? Was there any immediate danger of more falls? How much timber and what type of wood was required? How long would it take to secure the area once all the supplies have been gathered? Were there too many people in the vicinity of the fall area?

As I have said previously, I would never ask a man to do something I was afraid to do myself so on occasions like this I had to lead from the front. Once I had climbed on top of the supports I would be all alone in the bowels of the earth with only God and Lady Luck to protect me. My first task should have been to test for methane but because it was so important to get the roof secured as quickly as possible, this was almost always overlooked. What I normally did first was to erect some sort of temporary support immediately above the working area, if I could.

When conditions were this bad the only people allowed into the area would be the overman, a deputy and a couple of workmen. This would be all that was needed to do the job. The rest of the men would be sent to do other jobs or told to have their bait.

The machines and conveyors were all locked off and the place was filled with an uncanny silence. Once I had got on top of the supports the men passed up the timber and I began to build slowly and efficiently until the trellis work reached the roof. Once I had some semblance of support the atmosphere became much more relaxed. Usually, one of the other workers took over at this point and I let them get on with the job.

When roof conditions were good and the face was 'standing well' the chockmen had an easy time and were quite happy to do the job. When conditions changed and they had to dig out the chocks because the roof was flushing in, they thought that someone else should do it. 'This wouldn't have happened if them idiots in the other shift had timbered the roof properly,' they would cry. It's was always the other shift that did it wrong, never them!

The machine operators were no better. They always blamed the other shift for cutting too low or too high, or if the face conveyor was out of line. 'There's been no picks changed since I last changed them. There's still a leak in the hose that I reported to the fitter yesterday, the machine's going to stand still until it's put right. This is wrong, that's wrong.' And so the cry went on.

Having two machines on the face was more of a disadvantage than an advantage. No record was kept of how far the machines were shearing and, at one point, one end was so far in front of the other, tension built up and caused the AFC to undulate. Instead of being flat, the conveyor was all lumps and bumps causing all sorts of problems. With too much tension on the conveyor, when it was rammed forward it would automatically rise above the floor of the seam. In the circumstances, large wooden props were used as 'stays', forcing the conveyor on to the floor. However, this only transferred the problem further along the face and damaged the conveyor pans at the joints.

It was stupid to allow this system to operate as it only got the job done in the short term. But I was told that the men and officials had been doing it this way for over a decade and when I tried to explain to them that it was wrong I was the one considered to be stupid.

Continuing with my inspection I eventually reached the tail-gate end of the face. Two men were employed at the end of the face in much the same way as the men at the main entrance of the face. They also worked about only a third of their shift, depending on how many times the face had been cut.

Having already assessed what supplies were required by the chockmen I would instruct the two tail end men to go and get them. 'Not my job,' they would reply 'We haven't got the time.' 'Then make time,' I would tell them, and shortly I would have a dispute on my hands. Before I'd asked them to go and get the supplies they were sitting on their backsides waiting for their end of the face to be cut, and now they claimed to be so busy they didn't have time for anything else!!

As an official, I had to be very careful what I said to the workers. I quickly learned never to say to the men that they wouldn't get paid if they didn't do the job, 'Hey Charlie, the Deputy's not gan' a pay us.' Charlie would down tools and make his way to the nearest telephone with a loud hailing tannoy. 'The Deputy's stopped wor pay lads,' his voice would echo throughout the district and everyone would down tools and come off the face.

'We want to see a union man,' someone shouts and so a phone call is made to the union office at the surface. If they couldn't get in touch with the union secretary, or the union chairman or the deputy manager, they'd all walk out of the district and make their way to the surface, knowing full well that they would still get paid for the shift.

Disputes like this were quite common and you had to make a stand if you weren't going to let them get the better of you. After all it was the official's job to manage as well as uphold the law. I have known workers who were renowned for starting such disputes to go on eventually to become officials. It was all wrong, but it happened.

On a similar occasion, because two men were absent from work, I had to ask another two men to build a hardwood chock support to enable the machine to cut the face. It would have taken them only a few minutes to complete. However, they refused to do it, saying that it wasn't their job, knowing full well that the face couldn't be cut until the support had been built because of the manager's support regulations. I was furious to think that they would deliberately want to stop production and so, with the help of the overman, I started to build the support myself. At this, the men walked off the face and out of the pit. The men got paid and I was politely told to stop rocking the boat.

My inspection of the face almost complete, I would go to the tail-gate ripping lip. Here, four stonemen were employed to advance the tunnel. This was the worst job of all; they worked most of the shift in a dusty, noisy atmosphere shovelling stones. I felt sorry for them, and if anyone had the right to complain about their job they did. But the strange thing was that, at that particular time, they were the most easy going, conscientious set of workers you could wish for. And whatever they asked of me, if it was at all possible, I would do for them.

In some tail-gate roadways auxiliary fans were placed right next to where the stonemen were working. The fans were so noisy that the men had to use ear plugs to protect their hearing. With their ears bunged up, masks over their mouths and water constantly dripping on top of them, they were then expected to shovel stones for the entire shift. Ponies in the pre-war era probably worked in better conditions than these men, and we were supposed to be one of the most modern pits in Europe. It was just another example of how bad planning considerably reduced production. This would have been an ideal time to introduce the concept of retreat mining or pre-won roadways of the kind I had experienced at the Havannah and found to be the most productive, cost effective and safest form of mining because it dispensed with the intensive operations that were required at the face entrance and exit and (wastefully) employed many men.

A few yards from the ripping lip, and walking out bye (away from the face), I would come to a 50-yard long train that held the machinery that powered most of the equipment on the face. This included the electrically powered hydraulic pumps which supplied a lubricant to the powered support system. The train also housed a water tank used for dust suppression.

Here you might find two fitters and an electrician, the brains of the district. They were only required in an emergency during the production shift, but they were also required to keep the spare equipment in good condition. There was also a third semi-skilled fitter whose job was solely to look after the powered supports, repair hoses and defective rams, and check for leaks. Despite having the luxury of modern technology we didn't make best use of these men who were trained to deal with it.

Most of the wood supplies and arch girders were unloaded and stacked as near to the tail-gate ripping lip as possible. This was a problem as an incredible amount of wood was required for an advancing face. It made me wonder whether it would not be more profitable to sell the wood and leave the coal, as one worker put it.

When the face is advancing slowly the roof conditions tend to deteriorate and a break usually forms between the roof and the coalface. This is no problem at first, it's when the next strip of coal is taken out and the supports have to be advanced that the roof could cave in. Depending on the size of the fall, the timber supplies can quickly be used up, for example a week's supply of timber for an advancing face can be used up in one shift by a large roof fall.

Walking away from the face (outbye) down the tail-gate roadway, I would be always on the lookout for any deterioration of the roof and walls and making sure that there were no blockages in the water channel at the side of the road. At times, water ran off the face at a speed of 500 gallons a minute. As the roadway dipped away from the face, a small dam directed the flow of water into pipes and on to the main pumping station and from there it was pumped to the surface.

The tail-gate supply lads are always asking for the same things as their main-gate marras; more pay, a wet note, and an early finish. One of the lads here, however, went one better, he would always ask to change his afternoon shift on a Friday for day shift so that he could go out on Friday night. He tried it every time.

A 21-year-old lad came to me once and asked to change his shift because he had to appear in court. He had been divorced from his first wife and child, separated from his girlfriend and their child, and now he had got his third girlfriend in the family way. He had to go to court to sort out his maintenance. 'It's not a bloody shift change you want lad,' I said to him 'It's a week's holiday and a vasectomy operation.'

Having completed my inspection of the district I would arrive back at the kist. In a normal shift a deputy makes two inspections of his district and then writes out his report. One deputy (who shall remain nameless) once asked a young teenager how to spell heaven. The teenager promptly replied 'H.E.A.V.E.N. But what do you want to know that for?' he said. 'Well, you know as well as I do that we've been heaven trouble with the belts all shift.'

During one of my inspections, I came across two men on the coalface who were arguing about whose family had been the poorest when they were kids. Tommy said his family of nine had been so poor that for breakfast his Mam would tie a kipper on to a piece of string and hang it from the kitchen door, they were all given a piece of bread and on their way out they were allowed to slap the kipper with it. This was their bread and dripping! 'That's now't,' said Bill, 'We were so poor that on a Sunday we all took turns at wearing the only cap in the house to look out of the window.'

On another inspection a group of lads were sitting having their bait when I came across them. As usual the topic of conversation was sex. Each one was being asked if their wife was a virgin before she got married. An older man, sitting several yards away from the young lads, was asked the same question. After giving it some thought he turned to the lads and replied, quite seriously, 'No, she was an Armstrong from Jarrow I think.'

One of the most unpleasant things I had to do during one of my inspections was to give a dying man the 'kiss of life'. What made it more unpleasant was the fact that before he collapsed he had just been sick. It was awful, having to put my mouth to his after cleaning the sick from his mouth with only my fingers. At the Havannah, all of the officials were given proper appliances which fit around the patient's mouth, but at Westoe such things were frowned upon.

I carried out mouth-to-mouth resuscitation and a heart massage, but it was to no avail, he was dead. Somehow I felt that it was my fault that he'd died. I can still see the pleading look in his eyes just before he died, and even underneath all of that coal dust his face was so pale and sorrowful.

The next day I was told that even if he had been in hospital he would still have died, and I was to take comfort in the fact that I had done my best for him.

A few months later I nearly lost my own life due to an accident on the coalface. I was standing in the centre of the face between two powered supports looking first up the face and then down it, to check the alignment, when I noticed a wood support being carried along on the moving conveyor coming towards me and the cutting machine. As it got closer I leaned over to lift it from the conveyor when the coal seam, which was six-and-a-half feet high, collapsed, hitting me with a glancing blow to the back of my head forcing me on to the steel spill-plates of the conveyor belt.

The next thing I knew I was surrounded by voices and lights. I was half-dragged, half-carried on to the tail-gate and was only semi-conscious. After sitting me down on a wooden support my first reaction was to feel my brow. It was covered in bright red blood, my nose was all bunged up, and my eye felt as though it was six inches from my face.

The deputy arrived on the scene and began to examine my injuries. Although I felt groggy and was in terrible pain I could not help but laugh at his remarks. 'Oh God, What a mess, it's definitely broken,' referring, of course, to my nose. 'You're supposed to reassure the patient' I said.

'Oh, aye,' he replied, 'but I bet it's still broken.'

He was right. My nose was broken and my face was in a terrible mess with my left eye swollen and discoloured. To this day I still have a faint blue scar hidden by my eyebrow. Several weeks later I applied for compensation for my accident but I was told that, after an examination, my scar was not visible from a distance of six feet and therefore I would be given no compensation. I felt upset by the fact that what mattered was not my accident but whether anyone could see the scar – it didn't matter that I knew it was there.

On reflection, I was lucky to have escaped with just a scar. If I had been moving forward, instead of backwards, the overlapping coal would probably have knocked me on to the moving conveyor with my body most likely trapped beneath it. There I would have ended up under the shear loader and churned up like mincemeat mixed in with the coals.

In 1977 I was deputy of a district, and Tommy C. was the face overman. He reminded me of my older brothers; he was the same age as them and had the same hard-working attitude. If a certain face operation wasn't going to his liking he would take over the job himself and the men would take a back seat and watch him work.

Every shift Tommy would be on the go until the very last minute, and on several occasions he and I missed the train back to the shaft, making us up to two hours late by the time we got finished. 'No more running out at the last minute mind' I said to Tommy. 'OK,' he said. 'We'll give ourselves a few more minutes, John.'

Blow me if we didn't do the self same thing that following shift. Watching the train disappear into the distance my heart sunk into my boots. I looked at Tommy and he looked at me and we both burst out laughing. We got no extra pay for being late, just ridicule from our fellow officials, but that didn't bother us.

On another occasion, not only had we missed the train, but we also found the under-manager, who was in the same predicament. However, he told us not to worry as he knew a short cut which would get us out in less time. It was a bloody short cut alright, we ended up lost. 'Fancy,' I said to Tommy, 'an under-manager, a face overman and a deputy lost in a super pit.' 'For hell's sake don't tell anyone, John,' said Tommy, grinning.

The colliery overman of the district was Jack S. What a character he was. He reminded me a lot of Mr Rothery, the overman at Prestwick. He was also very short-tempered but had a sense of humour as well. He ruled his workers by fear. It's hard to imagine how a man so small could dominate a set of workers the way he did.

He'd surrounded himself with workers who were very loyal to him, and in all of my years in mining I had never experienced anything like it. They were of such a high calibre that if any job could be done, no matter how difficult, they would endeavour to do it for him. Quite often they would do things for Mr S. that any other worker wouldn't even attempt.

Jack and Fred D., the under-manager, had worked together in the early days when they both used to fill coal by hand on the conventional faces. Fred was a very religious man.

During one particular shift the rubber conveyor belt kept breaking and consequently very little coal was produced. The following day Jack said to Fred, 'Fred, do you think if we all prayed to the Good Lord above it would make any difference?' 'What do you mean?' asked Fred. 'Well, what with you being a kind of preacher, why not say a few prayers?' 'I can't do that down here,' replied Fred. 'I'll tell you what' said Jack, 'I'll get the lads to turn off their cap lamps so you won't be embarrassed.' Eventually, Fred agreed to do it and, at the kist, in complete darkness, Fred said a few prayers to the Good Lord asking him for his help and guidance. 'And do you know what happened?' said Jack. 'Not a bloody nut of coal was filled off that face during the whole bloody shift!'

Working underneath the North Sea meant that at times water seeped into the workings through the strata above. Sometimes the conditions were so bad that the face workers had to wear oilskins. However, after having worked a full shift with those on they were still soaking wet underneath, but due to perspiration not sea water.

Water not only made working conditions unpleasant, but when it started interfering with the conveyor belts it could wash the coals off causing all sorts of problems. What usually happened was that small coals choked the return roller and eventually broke the belt, stopping production for hours, shifts, or even days.

I worked in all kinds of atrocious conditions during my years in mining, but one of the worst shifts ever has to be what I called my 'Bloody Sunday'. I was driving to work that Sunday morning for the ten o'clock shift, one of the more civilised times of day to be travelling to work, when I overtook the village vicar on his way to mid-morning service. I waved at him and he waved back. 'Bloody Hell' I thought to myself, he's on his way to heaven and I'm on my way to hell!

Further on I was stopped by a police car and given a ticket for speeding at 45 miles per hour in a 30 mile per hour zone. Several weeks later I was fined £30, more than I was paid for working that shift.

For several days there had been roof falls in the middle of the face and so production had stopped. The fall had produced a cavity over 60 feet long and 12 feet wide, but no one could estimate the height as it was so large. The powered supports had been buried underneath the collapsed strata, which had also prevented the face chain conveyor from running.

My task was to try and free the conveyor and establish some kind of support for the roof. It was almost an impossible task but I had to try and make some headway.

Salt water was cascading down from the fall at such a speed that it was impossible to escape from it. No matter where you were working it spat at you as it bounced from the broken strata and collapsed supports. If you looked up at all you had to shade your eyes from the stinging salt water. It was like standing at the bottom of a ravine with sheer cliff faces on either side but it was much more dangerous as more strata could fall down on you at any minute without warning.

The normal face tunnel was completely blocked off, as was the tunnel under the powered supports. The only way through was to take your life in your hands and climb over the fall. To add to the misery, several of the hydraulic supports were defective and inoperable.

As an overman I had a deputy, three workmen, a fitter, and an electrician to assist me. On a Sunday afternoon there was only a skeleton staff at work. I decided that the first task was to bore holes in the largest stones and blast them with explosives in order to try and free the conveyor belt.

After having got all the necessary equipment ready, the men refused to work in such dangerous conditions, and I couldn't blame them. So, without saying another word, I took hold of the drill machine myself, with the feed electric cable dragging behind, and hauled myself and the machine over the collapsed supports, across the fall area and into such a position as to enable me to bore the holes. Eventually, without being asked, one of the workers climbed into the area and gave me a hand. I was very grateful for his help as it usually takes two people to put some beef into the drilling operation.

To bore the necessary holes I had to place myself in all sorts of difficult positions, sometimes lying on my back with the machine on top of me, sometimes lying on my side, sometimes kneeling or even crouching. All the time the salt water was running up my sleeve, or down my neck, or into my wellingtons – no way could I escape from it. After we had completed the boring operation we were soaking wet and must have looked like a couple of drowned rats. Seeing the terrible state we were in, the deputy had the cheek to suggest there was no need for him to get into the same state and would we mind charging and stemming the drill holes for him. I had to laugh. 'OK' I said, 'pass over the detonators and explosives.'

Once the large stones had been fired, after some initial difficulty we managed to free the AFC and 40 to 50 tons of coal and stones poured off the face. My plan had been a success. Not only had I freed the coal, we were now able to pass through the face tunnel.

Several minutes later a second fall occurred, in exactly the spot where we had been working. Had the second fall occurred just a few minutes earlier I have no doubt that we would have been killed instantly. The falls of stone were so large that we would have probably have had to be scraped off them. And now I had to start the job all over again!

Fortunately the job was much easier because we had cleared the face tunnel earlier on. We drilled more holes in the second fall and, after blasting, the face conveyor was freed once again.

At that particular time, having to work in such terrible conditions was quite common and very little production was gained. Sometimes whole shifts were taken up with digging out the supports. And on several occasions all your time was spent in the same area of the face, because the hydraulic rams, which are attached to the supports, had to be advanced up the conveyor before production could begin.

When I worked on the low mechanised faces at the Havannah I used to dream about working on seven-feet-high faces and wonder what it must be like. Well now I knew! At times, conditions were much worse on the high seams and I still had to crawl along the face on my elbows. I never thought I'd have to do that at Westoe.

One of the most hated jobs at the coalface was replacing a damaged or defective 250-yard-long, semi-armoured, electric trailing cable, which powered the cutting machine. The moment a cable became damaged production was halted. This used to infuriate me because it was usually due to neglect that the cable became damaged in the first place; after all, one man was permanently assigned to looking after the cable.

It was the electrician's job to discover whereabouts the cable had been damaged, and then to condemn it. Damaged cables, if left in place, had a history of causing a lot of underground explosions as the sparks from a damaged cable had enough intensity to ignite any methane gas that might have been present.

As the electrician was examining the cable, it was the official's job to arrange for the defective cable to be removed from the face and sent out to the area workshops to be repaired, and, in the meantime, replace it with a spare cable. The cost of having to replace a damaged cable underground must have been astronomical when you consider what it involved: the financial cost of lost production; transport facilities to the surface; transport from the colliery to area workshops, and back again; the cost of repair; and the cost to have the repaired cable transported back underground to be stored as a spare.

An electrical engineer once told me that during the life of the face, up to 98 cables could be reported damaged. This represents, on average, one cable a week, which I thought was an absolute disgrace. On a later face this figure was reduced from 98 to two!

At that time it was quite common for some officials to take no steps to remove the damaged cable. Instead, they only concentrated on getting a new cable installed. In the long term this action was detrimental to production and having two cables on the face caused all sorts of problems. Often you could end up with two damaged cables almost one after the other.

At the beginning of one particular shift, production was standing because a damaged cable had been left from the previous shift. Not only that, but the tunnelling machine in the advance heading (the hollow chamber maintained in advance of the face) also had a damaged cable.

Having told the three advance heading workers how to replace the cable to the tunnelling machine, I was free to concentrate on replacing the face cable and get production moving again. The problem was so urgent that the deputy manager came along to assist me. The roof conditions throughout most of the face had deteriorated, making the job more difficult as much of the cable had been buried underneath roof falls.

The deputy manager and myself were sweating profusely and getting quite exhausted due to the effort involved, when suddenly a voice came blasting out of the loud hailing system, 'Come in John Graham, come in John Graham.' I was lying on my side, wedged between a pile of stones and the powered roof support tunnel, trying to free the cable. The reply box was also buried underneath the rubble, but after shifting several large stones, I was eventually able to press the operating button and answer the call.

'This is the general manager,' a voice came booming out of the speaker. 'What bloody idiot organised this cable job?' 'I did,' I replied. 'I don't think much of your organisation, you've got the whole district standing!' he shouted. (At this point we were at cross purposes, each referring to different jobs). 'The district's been standing since the beginning of the shift, or were you not aware of what's happening in your bloody pit?'

By now I was furious. Being called a 'bloody idiot' by the general manager over the tannoy system which was echoed all around the district was like waving a red flag to a raging bull. It was an insult I could not stomach. The deputy manager, who was lying on his side trying to crawl over the stones that choked the powered support tunnel, tried to tell me to calm down. 'There's no bugger going to call me a bloody idiot and get away with it,' I told him.

I started to crawl away down the face. 'Where are you going?' shouted the deputy manager. 'I'm going to see that bugger now,' I replied. I eventually made my way off the face and down to the main road entrance, where I met a fellow official from another district. 'Where's the general manager?' I asked. 'You've just missed him John, he's gone to bank.' 'Bloody hell,' I thought in exasperation, 'Just my luck.'

Just then the three other workers I had sent to seek the new cable arrived on the scene. 'Where the bloody hell have you idiots been all this time?' I enquired. They all looked sheepish. 'They're the culprits who have been stopping and starting the conveyor,' said the development official. 'WHAT!' I exploded. 'Who gave you the permission to use the conveyors?' I demanded. 'Nobody' came the reply. 'But we thought it would be quicker 'cause the transport train was derailed.'

The official then told me exactly what had happened. The general manager, who had been visiting a new face installation on the low side of the district, was being transported out of the district on the man-riding conveyor. However, the conveyor was being stopped and started all the while as the men were seeing to their cable. The conveyor stopped and the general manager stood up to get off just when the conveyor started up again. He hit his head on an overhead cable which dislodged a stone dust barrier and covered him from head to foot in limestone dust. He was furious at having to walk out of the district due to the faulty conveyor and being covered in dust did not help his mood!

When he reached the main trunk line and found out why the conveyor kept being interrupted, he contacted me. He obviously thought that I had organised the cable job using the conveyor, which was just not so. I played hell with the three lads. 'Do you bloody idiots realise that not only have you managed to stop production from the developments, but you got me a bollocking from the general manager, and you've disrupted his schedule for the rest of the day by making him walk half a mile out of the district when he could have had a ride?' 'Sorry John,' said one of the lads, 'But it couldn't have happened to a nicer chap.' We all burst out laughing. 'Bugger off and get your machine going, it's stood for long enough.' Although it was serious, I couldn't help seeing the funny side of it.

They had just disappeared out of sight, when the young transfer point attendant at the main-gate entrance stood on a moving haulage rope and went over on his ankle. With help, I quickly bandaged him up and stretchered him to the surface. 'Bloody hell' I thought, 'It's just not my day.'

I accompanied the patient to the medical centre and then went to see my under-manager. I explained to him about the young lad twisting his ankle, but I also told him that my main reason for coming to the surface was to have it out with the general manager. No one was going to call me a 'bloody idiot' and get away with it, especially when all the workers could hear him as well. He could shove the pit up his backside for all I was concerned.

The under-manager told me to calm down, go and have a shower, and he would ring through to the general manager's office and make me an appointment to see him. This I did.

Returning from the shower, I approached the main office. His secretary looked up at me, 'Yes. Can I help you?' 'I want to see the general manager.' 'Have you got an appointment?' 'Yes. Just tell him John Graham is here to see him.' This she did, and then told me that he would see me now. Suddenly I began to feel terribly nervous. 'What am I doing here?' I thought. I was beginning to lose my confidence. But I was determined I was not going to let him get away with it. After all, I was in the right, and when I'm right, I'm never afraid of anyone. 'Just remember John,' I said to myself, 'Look him straight in the eyes and stare him out.'

I knocked on the door, there was no answer. I knocked again, still no answer so I went marching in. The manager, sitting behind his desk, looked up at me while knocking the tobacco from his pipe into an ash tray, but still he never spoke. 'I'm John Graham and I think you owe me an apology.' At the same time I banged the door shut. He looked at me straight in the eyes and told me to sit down, motioning to one of the chairs.

'Nobody calls me a "bloody idiot". Not you, not even the chairman, Sir Derek Ezra.' He stopped me before I could say anything else, and then proceeded to tell me all the problems he had in running a large colliery employing 2,400 men.

We sat and chatted for almost half an hour. He asked me about my previous mining experience, he enquired about my former collieries, and he asked me what I thought about Westoe. I told him that I thought the potential was there but that the men's attitude was all wrong.

At the end of our discussion he asked me about the patient that I had brought to the medical centre. 'After all, that's why you came out early isn't it?' he said with a gleam in his eye. I looked at him and thought, by God, you're a hard man, but fair, and yet the bugger still didn't apologise. Then he said 'Well lad, one – thank you for having the courage to come knocking on my door, two – for fighting your own battles instead of involving the union, three – maybe you did get the short end of the stick underground, and four – I can assure you that no harm will come to you because of this experience, only good. Good day to you.'

I left his office feeling ten feet tall. At last I felt part of Westoe. Most of the officials looked up in awe at the colliery manager, in fact, we considered him to be some kind of demi-god. The next day men came up to me and shook my hand, saying that they had heard about what I had done and they were proud of me. It was a really marvellous feeling to be so popular, especially when before they had never trusted me. Isn't life funny?

In the late sixties, during Lord Robens' era, a film was made by the NCB called 'Nobody's Face'. It was used internally for the benefit of officials, workmen and mechanics and it highlighted how silly mistakes could interfere with production. Its main message was that efficiency could be greatly increased by increasing understanding and co-operation amongst the men. At Westoe most faces were nobody's!

The late seventies was one of the most frustrating periods during the whole of my working life at the coalface. The men would just not co-operate. They used any excuse they could to delay or stop production. Men would deliberately lock-off the conveyors on the pretext of safety. It reached such a point that to get the machine to run for a whole hour meant you'd achieved something.

I knew from experience that the quicker the rate of advance of the face the safer the roof conditions, usually. I also knew that the face must be kept as straight as possible, and at 90 degrees to the roadway. You can never put enough emphasis on the importance of keeping the face straight. As a young lad under-cutting the coal I knew just how much it meant to keep the face straight. But this cannot be achieved by guess work and good luck. It can only be achieved by correct measurement. However, for some reason the use of a tape measure to record daily advances at Westoe was frowned upon, it was only used at weekends to measure the weekly advance. The straightness of the face was guess work and, due to this, I once recorded a difference of some 17 yards between the two ends of a face.

I have always believed that prevention is better than cure, and time and again this principle was proved at Westoe. Having a face out of line meant that the conveyor was forced to undulate instead of running straight and caused all sorts of unnecessary problems. Competency was measured not on how much coal you were able to produce, but how quickly you could repair a breakdown that should never have occurred in the first place.

We officials were as much to blame as anyone else as there was no co-ordination between shifts. Each shift got what it could and bugger the rest. There was never any harmony, and attitudes were all negative. I failed to get the message across to my fellow officials on the importance of keeping the face straight and I got the impression that senior management wasn't bothered either.

The potential to achieve huge tonnages was there, but the attitude of getting the machines to cut at all costs, no matter how unaligned the face, stood in the way and meant that long-term productivity was severely hampered. Each shift thought they knew what was best and there was never any continuity.

It didn't help that we now had a cohort of men that had started to work in the mines just before the 1972 strike. Their attitude to the job was totally wrong; they believed that when it came to the crunch they could get away with anything. 'After all we brought down the Government' was a phrase commonly used by the workers.

The face workers had no respect for the officials and vice versa. I would be a very rich man indeed if I had been given a pound for every time someone threatened to take me to the union. Although I had acquired a very bad name among some of the workers, I never let this bother me. All I wanted to do was get the job done.

The workings in the 5/4 seam were bisected by the main trunk roads which practically divided the seam into two distinct areas; the North side seam and the South side seam. The South side was worked by the retreat method of mining and the North side by the advancing method.

The retreat method is the best method possible as the face workings advance towards the main trunk belts instead of away from them, as in the case of the advancing system. Using the retreat method, two parallel tunnels are driven, 250 yards apart and over 1,000 yards into the coal seam. The two roads are joined at the end by a connecting road, also in the seam. This connecting road becomes the new face line.

During this project a new team of men came into the district; they had previously been working in another part of the mine but that was now exhausted. They were older than the other men and much more experienced.

They had been used to working the piece rate system and their attitude was like a breath of fresh air.

At this time a new powered support was installed on the face. I was curious to know the cost of the new supports as it was rumoured to have gone into thousands. The management would never tell us exactly how much they cost, but one of the reps told me that they were something in the region of £1,000 per ton. Each powered support weighed 12 tons so must have cost £12,000! I couldn't believe it, they must have contained gold somewhere in their structure for them to cost that much. Each powered support cost the equivalent of a new car, and an expensive one at that, and there were 156 supports required on this face.

The usual method of payment for powered roof supports was a hire system from the area plant pool, and the colliery was charged rental on a weekly basis. However, these supports werea prototype and rumour had it that they were too expensive for the plant pool system, but they were intended to have a life span of at least a decade.

After getting used to the new supports I decided they were the best I had ever encountered – and so they should be at that price. They meant that you virtually had a roof of steel from one end of the face to the other. As well as being stronger than the original powered supports, they had the added advantage of a pressure gauge, which at least gave some indication as to whether or not the supports were doing their job.

In the past supports had no gauge fitted and quite often they would lower off for no apparent reason. This helped to induce breaks in the roof leading to an eventual roof fall. Working with faulty supports made the job even more dangerous, especially when conditions were already bad, for example when they had to support a timbered cavity after a roof fall.

Some reasonable results were achieved under the retreat system, but two weeks of good production would be followed by a week of very little because the alignment of the face had been ignored for the previous couple of weeks and had to be put right.

The problem as I saw it was that in order to maintain full employment six faces were being worked, so at times the colliery was overproducing, but the conveying system could not cope with peak loading periods. This meant that men and machines were standing idle at the coalface due to the over capacity, but as the colliery output was easily maintained no one appeared to be bothered.

In 1979 we entered the new era of incentive payments and left behind the day-wage system. Some men started to grasp the carrot, or incentive, and attitudes began to change for the better. But some workers, especially the younger element, were still sceptical of the incentive bonus. Some men were so used to having a 'couldn't care less' attitude that they just weren't ready for the change.

In the eyes of the union all men are equal and in mining this meant that they were entitled to do face work if they so desired. Travelling through the face on one particular occasion I came across a workman lowering, advancing and resetting one of the powered supports. But instead of resetting it tightly against the roof, the support was only partly engaged and so not doing its job properly.

When I challenged him as to why he was not fitting it correctly he said 'You'll get a bloody ulcer worrying like that.' As far as I was concerned the man should not have been allowed anywhere near the coalface. However, after reporting the incident, I was told that I couldn't take him off the job as he could claim it was victimisation!

At times, men working on modern mechanised faces were reluctant to set supports properly because, in their opinion, it broke up the roof. Trying to educate the men to understand how to do it the right way was like hitting your head on a brick wall.

To overcome the 'idiot problem' the Coal Board, at great expense, fitted a constant pressure hydraulic system to the powered supports. This means that each individual support was of uniform strength. The cost – a mere £120,000 plus labour. To me, this expense was unnecessary; all the situation required was common sense. But it seems that idiots have to be protected from themselves and so the supports were made idiot proof.

In 1981 an Indian scientist called Ramma came underground at Westoe to carry out scientific experiments in strata control. He was very brave, dedicated and conscientious.

The under-manager introduced me to Ramma and asked me to see that he got all the assistance he needed to carry out his experiments. (His thesis was later presented at Newcastle University). His main tasks were to drill and bore holes in the strata above and below the coal seam, and in the coal seam itself. He then measured and recorded the cracks stemming from the holes due to natural convergence. He also recorded the different pressures on the powered supports.

At times he had to be very quick, to make sure that his experiments didn't interfere with production. I assigned a workman to help him. At first the workmen were a bit sceptical of him because they didn't like the way he always set the powered supports at a constant pressure – they still believed it broke up the roof. Thankfully, after a while they came to admire him, even though he quite often got in the way. I always made sure he got his work completed, even if it did occasionally mean delaying production for a few minutes.

The under-manager later told me that Ramma's experiments had proved that after the weekends, when no production was undertaken, the total length of the coalface moved towards the conveyor. This contradicted the previously held belief that pressure moved the conveyor and powered supports towards the coalface. (The first shift often found the conveyor rammed tight against the face and could never understand why.) Ramma eventually returned to an academic life in India.

Trying to get the young men who worked at the pit to change their ways was an ongoing problem. They claimed to be frightened of no one, saying that even Mrs Thatcher's government backed down in 1981 after confronting them. 'There's a day of reckoning coming,' I was constantly preaching to them, but they never took a blind bit of notice.

If, on the first day of the week, production was low due to delays, the men would lose heart and throw in the towel for the rest of the week. Attitudes would quickly deteriorate and we were soon back to the 'couldn't care less' feeling. To get them to work at all was very difficult.

Disputes underground between the men and me were frequent. I had to keep making a stand to prove that I was in charge and to demonstrate that I had the right to manage. 'If only you would do the correct thing by keeping the face straight and not cheat by taking extra cuts off the ends, conditions would improve,' I kept telling them. It was as effective as whispering in a howling gale. I seemed to be the only person who believed that the coal was down there to be brought out, safely, efficiently and economically. No one else seemed give a damn whether coal was brought out or not.

My feelings at times like this were so low that my home life suffered because of them. Getting out of bed at 2am, travelling 30 miles by car to work and then a further six miles underground out into the North Sea, and spending another five hours trying to get men to do something they didn't want to do was enough to drive a man crazy. I would return home so tired and frustrated that if my wife even looked at me the wrong way I would bite her head off.

My dream of achieving excellence had turned sour. The potential of Westoe was obvious, yet I felt helpless. No one, not even senior management, appeared to be bothered or even interested. Output was easily maintained because there were six faces at the pit.

As I saw it, one of the main problems was not geological but human error. Cutting the coalface and grading the roof and floor of the seam was left to different people. On some occasions six to eight workmen could cut the same face in 24 hours and each one had their own idea of how it should be cut. Uniformity, attention to detail, and pride was absent from their work.

Trying to stamp my authority on such matters made relations with the machine operators highly volatile at times. It was common for them to stop the machine and walk off the face. But at all times I knew I was right and I kept persevering in my quest for perfection at the coalface. Something inside me kept telling me to persist, persist, persist ...

Towards the end of 1981 my dream was realised. A new, 250-yard advancing production face had been installed with a modern double-ranging arm, single shearer loading machine. The powered supports used were the first ones to be fitted with pressure gauges so that you had a visual indication of what pressure was being applied to the setting load, and you also knew what pressure was being applied to the supports by the overlying strata.

Years earlier I had been told by several officials and workmen that it was a hopeless task to try and mine the North side of the district, the only good results in the past had been achieved on the South side.

Here I was presented with the chance to put all my experience and theories into practice. I was given a brand new face all to myself. Because of certain circumstances I was told that the face would only be producing one shift a day; that meant that the machine would only operate for five hours (shift time at the face) in every 24 hours, and only one team of men would cut the face and advance the supports.

I was to be the overman responsible for the efficiency of everything and everyone in that shift. At the time I thought it was strange that senior management should even think about installing a face with equipment worth more than £2 million and yet decide to put it into production for only five hours a day, five days a week. Perhaps I was being used as a guinea pig for technology. The manager of Westoe colliery was now a man I had worked for at Havannah when he was a young under-manager on his first assignment.

Twelve men were cavilled to the face during the production shift – these men were the coal producers – and there was another team of three men assigned to the main road advance heading, 15 men in total. A further eight men, four in each roadway, advanced the two roadways but they worked in a different shift to the coal producers.

The cutter-loader machine was of the latest design, and comparing it to the machines I had previously used was like comparing Rolls Royce to a Mini. It had two large cutting and loading discs at each end of the main body and its overall length was some 32 feet. It was a real monster.

At the touch of a button you could raise or lower each disc and place it into any position in relation to the coal seam. It was mounted on to the conveyor and pulled itself along the coalface by means of a 30 millimetre haulage chain. The haulage chain stretched from one end of the face to the other and anchored itself on to the end of the conveyor.

When a new face began production it took a while for the seam to 'soften'. Usually the coal was so hard to begin with that, after every cut of the face, cutting picks had to be replaced. The rate of advance was slow and it took about 30 yards of face advance before the waste area behind the powered supports collapsed. Air that should have been travelling along the face tunnel found its way into the waste area. This decreased the amount of air and, therefore, the speed at which it travelled in the face tunnel and this led to a build up of airborne dust. There was not much you could do about this other than good housekeeping, making sure that the air was guided onto the face tunnel by placing special cloths at certain points to direct the air flow. As the face advanced and the goaf area began to collapse behind the powered supports, a natural tunnel was formed for the ventilation.

Owing to the hardness of the coal seam, the shearer-loader could not achieve its maximum potential, and so during this initial period, which lasted several weeks, the men could only manage to earn the colliery average incentive bonus. However, when the seam began to soften up, the men were paid by their own face incentive which was agreed between the NUM and management. The seam was softened up by the increasing pressure of the strata above it.

The face team was made up of mostly middle-aged men; three of them were in their late fifties and were waiting for their redundancy notices. Most of them were good, old-fashioned pitmen used to conventional methods of mining and knew what it was all about. They had a different attitude to the management and were more conscientious than the younger element. However, having over a decade of experience on mechanised faces, some of them did not take kindly to being supervised. They were used to having their own way.

The normal incentive achieved was two-and-a-half shears per shift, that is, two-and-a-half cuts off the full length of the face. Each cut had to be to a depth of two feet and the advance was measured in lineal meters. The first two weeks of face advance, at the incentive norm of two-and-a-half cuts, was below average and their bonus was just over £3 a shift.

Relations with the men were quite strained as I was always at them to do the right thing. On this particular shift I went onto the face and found that they had taken an extra cut off the end of the face and this had put the face out of line. Their reason for doing this was to get an extra measurement at the end of the face, without having to cut the whole length of the face, to get a bigger bonus. But all they were doing was cheating and the extra cuts would have to be taken off the middle of the face before long. It was just plain stupid.

The next day, at the beginning of the shift, I got them all together and would not allow them on to the face until I had had a word with them. 'Do you want to make money?' was my first question. 'Of course we do. What do you think we're here for?' came the reply. 'Then why don't you do the correct thing, instead of trying to cheat all the time? If anything goes wrong, we only have ourselves to blame. From now on, you're going to do things my way. Properly and correctly, without cheating.' 'Oh Aye! Mr Know-it-all. I've been doing this job before you were pupped,' said one of the men. 'Yes. And just look at the state of the face, it's out of line and in a right mess,' I said. 'Well, if you can do any better, get on with it,' said another.

I decided it was no good getting their backs up and tried and calm them down as they were all beginning to get agitated and aggressive. But I had to persuade them into my way of thinking.

'Look here, we've got a glorious opportunity to make a name for ourselves and for you lot to make some money,' I said. 'Let's change our priorities, we'll put the face before anything else and make conditions on the face as good as is humanly possible.' 'How do we do that then? We haven't got a magic wand.' 'Well, we can do it if we all change our attitudes. Let's just give it a week's trial. I'll keep the face as straight as possible – all you have to do is everything I ask you to do. I guarantee you'll be better off.' 'We've got nowt to lose. Let's give the bugger a chance,' said Vinegar Smith.

One of the key jobs on a mechanised face was ramming forward the conveyor whenever the face advanced. The man cavilled to this job was Hugh M., a 58-year-old just waiting for his redundancy. Hugh had never done this job before so I suggested that I would get one of the other lads

to swap jobs with him. 'Oh no John,' said Hughie, 'I want to learn.'
'That's grand Hughie' I said to him. 'You just do everything I ask of you
and don't take notice of anyone but me.'

Another key job, the most obvious, was operating the cutter loader
machine. The two men detailed to this job, Norman S. and John T., were
probably as good at this job as anyone else at Westoe. Their approach to
the job was old fashioned in that John was the number one operator and
Norman, number two. John always took the leading end and cut and
graded the roof, while Norman did the floor. If any error occurred in the
roof or the floor, each man knew who was responsible.

I supervised Hughie closely, and showed him how I wanted the
conveyor lined up. The face alignment is of paramount importance. In
the past, the men had been used to the twin shearer that had two cutters
and loaders, one at each end of the face, and the alignment tended to be
neglected. This was mainly due to pressure from senior management
always taking a short term view in their quest for production.

Aligning the face is a simple, straightforward job, but somehow the
simplest of jobs took a lot of getting across to fellow officials and the
other workers. Ramming forward the AFC a couple of inches, as part of
the alignment, means that the powered supports can only be advanced by
the same two inches. To the men, this seemed stupid, but, they did all
that I asked of them, despite voicing their displeasure.

Someone must have told the colliery overman that they were
advancing the powered supports by a couple of inches instead of the
customary 24 inches per cut. He asked me what the hell I was doing, and
so I explained my plans. 'You'll lose coal that way,' he said. 'Yes,' I
replied, 'but it is the most important cut in order to get the face
alignment correct.'

Eventually I got my way and production increased in leaps and
bounds. John T. came up to me and said that he'd never seen face
conditions so good. 'Why not make conditions even better by helping the
tail-gate stonemen?' I suggested. 'How do you mean, John?' 'By letting

the machine cut and load the stones at the tail-gate and by profiling the roadway and, therefore, eliminating most of the drilling, blasting and shovelling.' 'I've tried this once before in the Brass Thill seam and it didn't work, it took up too much time,' said John. 'If you do it my way,' I suggested, 'it will take only a few extra seconds.' 'OK' said John, 'I'll give it a try.'

He did as I asked and it turned out to be a huge success. It meant that the tail-gate stoneman had very little shovelling to do and instead of setting one steel arch girder per shift, they sometimes managed to set up to four.

The three men working the development machine in the advance heading had to get their fingers out. Instead of them advancing the headway by one yard per shift, they would have to manage three or four. Not only did they do this, they also assisted in the main road work when necessary. Their attitudes also changed, from being downright lazy, they were now hard working and conscientious.

Eventually, all the men's attitudes changed. Conditions became so good that coal poured off the face at over 300 tons an hour, 1,500 tons in one shift! And the face incentive bonus rose from £3 per shift to £25, adding up to a bonus of £125 per week for the facemen. It was not a flash in the pan either; this rate of production continued shift after shift, week after week, month after month. My dream had come true. My relationship with the men was second to none, I became their champion and in their eyes I could do no wrong.

Conditions were so good that the men who were due to take their redundancy were beginning to have second thoughts. Tommy C. and Billy L. both told me that, having worked in the mines all of their lives, they had never imagined in their wildest dreams that working on a coalface could be so pleasant, safe and rewarding, and it made a mockery of Arthur Scargill's blood on the coal theory as accidents throughout the district were non-existent.

Geordie O., who worked on the tail-gate roadway and was used to

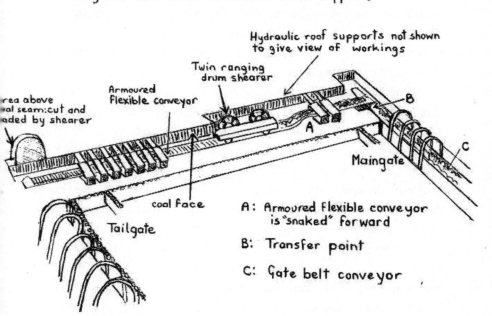

POWER LOADING - TWIN RANGING DRUM SHEARER
Longwall coal face 2 metres thick (approx)

Hydraulic roof supports not shown to give view of workings

Twin ranging drum shearer

Armoured Flexible conveyor

rea above al seam:cut and aded by shearer

B

A

C

Maingate

coal face

Tailgate

A: Armoured flexible conveyor is "snaked" forward

B: Transfer point

C: Gate belt conveyor

shovelling a mountain of stones all shift, said he never thought he would see the day when his job was made so much easier. Everyone became involved. Face delays due to machine failure were eliminated, a decade of bad practices came to an end, mechanical breakdowns were rare, and cables seemed to last forever. The two cutting discs stayed in a fixed position and only rarely did the men need to adjust them.

I had realised my dream of achieving excellence on the coalface and I felt very proud. Shining my spotlight along the coalface and seeing the powered supports standing to attention with military precision, and watching coals come pouring from the face like a black river was a real joy. Of course, there were the sceptics who thought that I was lucky to have such good face conditions and never gave me any credit at all. I soon quietened them down when a four-foot displacement (fault) appeared in the coal seam at the main road end of the face and gradually it worked its way along the face. The displacement first looked as if it would really slow down production. 'That's buggered it,' remarked one of the facemen, 'We'll make nowt now.' 'Not at all,' I said 'There's no reason why we can't maintain the same rate of production provided we maintain the same standards.'

I'd noticed that the strata above and below the coal seam at the displacement area was as hard as the coal. Providing that the newly exposed roof was immediately controlled, and the armoured conveyor was graded correctly, there was no reason why the fault should hold up production. The eventual production results proved that my theory had been correct. And what pleased me most was the fact that we had graded the conveyor using the machine instead of reverting to the terrible habit of forcing the conveyor down using wooden props as stays.

Another problem that I managed to overcome was that of 'face creep'. Keeping the face conveyor at right angles to both roadways and their respective centre lines was simple as there was no other official to have to argue my point of way with.

In the past, the Coal Board had gone to great lengths to try and overcome the problem of face creep by creating and installing massive anchor stations but they proved ineffective. Face creep was caused by bad management, taking strips of coal off one end of the face because preparations had not been completed at the other end.

Having the courage to take your orders from the situation, and always looking to the long term, not only benefited the men, it also benefited the face and, in turn, the colliery. To keep the face line straight, after every tenth cut I would ram forward the conveyor using the haulage chain as a guideline, having first of all checked the measurements of advance and making sure that the conveyor had not crept to the left or to the right in relation to both road tunnel centre lines. To my delight, there was no face creep.

The face was being cut, on average, four-and-a-half times a shift, twenty plus times a week, so at least twice a week I could 'shear to line' to keep the face straight. This meant that instead of following the gradient of the coal, the machine would shear off a straight line. The men, who were very sceptical of this practice at first, now loved it and would refer to it as a 'quickie', as the machine could travel at its maximum speed of 30 feet per minute as against the normal 16. During every shift they would ask 'If there any I chance of a quickie John?' Life was indeed sweet, but I felt that in no way did my earnings match my efforts, as I was not on the same incentive bonus as the men were! However, I did feel extremely proud to be managing the face properly at last, my way.

I was now in the unique position of having worked on faces producing 1,000 tons a week at Prestwick, to 1,000 tons a day at Havannah, and then 1,500 to 1,700 tons per shift at Westoe. I was now personally responsible for producing 7,500 tons of coal a week, 375,000 tons a year. The pithead price per ton was £40. This meant that I was financially responsible for producing £60,000 worth of coal in one shift, £300,000 worth a week, and a staggering £15,000,000 worth a year. It was indeed progress, men and machines pulling together to achieve what was thought of a few years earlier as the impossible, and in only 300 minutes of day, five days a week.

Face conditions were further improved by the introduction of a coal thickness indicator (CTI). This was a radio-active gamma sensor confined in a steel box and secured to the top of the cutting machine. The NCB Mining Research Department developed the sensor to detect very weak emissions of radiation given off by thorium, potassium and uranium which are present in the shales that overlie the coal seams. ('Bloody hell.' I thought, 'Radiation! That can cause cancer.' Did it contribute to miners dying from cancer? I wondered.)

The idea was for this instrument to give more accurate assessment of the amount of coal that had been left behind, after the seam had been extracted, to form the roof. For example, if the seam was six-and-a-half feet thick, six feet of coal would be extracted, leaving half a foot of coal to form the roof; it was known as roof coal. Until this machine had been invented, there was no way of knowing exactly how much coal was being left behind.

The CTI had to be placed underneath the roof of coal, where there was known to be approximately six inches of coal left. A hole would then be drilled in the roof to ascertain the exact thickness of coal that had been left behind. The assistant electrical engineer would then calibrate the sensor. It could reliably detect between 0 and 18 inches of roof coal.

The roof coal thickness was transmitted to an indicator unit secured at the side of the machine. The information was displayed in the form of lights. When the roof coal was of the desired thickness, the central bar lit up, however if the coal was too thick, red lights would shine, and if the coal roof was too thin, yellow lights would light up. Each light represented an increase or decrease in the coal roof of two centimetres.

As soon as the CTI was attached to the machine I couldn't wait to try it out. It worked perfectly. But now I had the job of explaining to the men how the machine worked. They found the metric measurements a bit confusing but as far as they were concerned, red meant danger, and I told them that that is all they had to worry about.

I had now proved that higher production didn't mean that there had to be blood on the coal. In fact, just the opposite was true; better results were achieved by creating conditions that were as perfect as possible. Better face conditions also reduced the incidence of injuries and accidents. In fact, I was now beginning to realise that the conditions I had now created could have benefited the ROLF system that Lord Robens tried to introduce in the late sixties whereby coal production on the face was operated by remote control.

With proper organisation, a retreat system of mining, and reasonable face conditions, I knew that one production unit, more intensively mined, could produce the entire colliery's output worth around of £1.2 million a week. Westoe had to change sometime. The colliery could become a gold mine not a coal mine!

Technology was being introduced at an alarming rate, so fast in fact, that often the miners were not even aware of it themselves. On a whitewashed brick wall at the main road entrance, a small, white steel box had been placed with several black cables coupled to it. I asked the electrician, who happened to be working nearby, what it was for. He opened up the box and revealed several rows of small electrical lights. By pressing individual buttons small red lights appeared on a display board; each light represented a different piece of machinery such as the armoured conveyor, the stage loader, or one of the many conveyors operated along the main road. If, after pressing one of the switches, no red light appeared it meant that that particular piece of machinery was not working.

This was a piece of technology to be marvelled at. Although I was several hundred yards from the shearer loader, by pressing one of these buttons I could tell whether or not the machine was working.

Placed next to the installation box was a tannoy phone which enabled me to speak directly to the face workers if and when production was delayed. From here I could then give them instructions to get production started again. This was all part of the computerised system that had been recently installed and was referred to by the acronym FIDO. (Face information digested on line).

This system provided senior management with up-to-the-minute information on the state of all six faces. A visual display unit in their offices showed whether or not the shearer was cutting coal, or whether the conveyors were working, or whether the face supports were in order. Armed with this data, senior management could make instant decisions without even going underground, saving both time and money – well, that was the idea. But the way I looked at it, in the near future these machines would make my job redundant.

The control centre at the surface was immediately informed of any breakdown of machines. This meant that those in the control room could give instructions on how to repair the breakdown before the officials had even got to the scene. In fact, on some occasions, senior management at the surface were made aware of a breakdown even before the underground official.

After the electrician showed me how to work this little white box, I found it to be a very valuable asset, especially when I was one of the very few people who knew what it was. Fellow officials and other workmen were mystified as to how I could tell as soon as a machine had been switched off when I was nowhere near it.

I remember on one occasion, having just reached the main road transfer point, I noticed that there were no coals on the conveyors. I checked with the white box and found that all the small red lights were lit. I knew, therefore, that all the conveyors were running and it would just be a matter of time before the stream of coals arrived.

Just then the shift under-manager arrived on the scene and immediately grew concerned by the fact that there were no coals on the conveyor. 'What's wrong?' he said. 'I'm buggered if I know,' I replied, showing no signs of concern whatsoever. The look of astonishment on his face was a sight to behold. 'What are you going to do about it?' he enquired. 'Bugger all,' I answered. 'I suggest you go in there and see what's wrong,' he said, rather angrily. 'Go yourself, I've already been on to the face and conditions were OK.'

By now the colour was really draining from his cheeks – he just couldn't understand my total lack of concern. Just then the coals started pouring from the conveyor chute and on to the main trunk conveyor. I burst out laughing and then showed him how I knew production was standing. He called me all the bloody idiots he could think of, but it was all part of mining humour.

My 250-yard, single shift production face was now advancing at a rate of over 40 feet a week. My daily tasks of checking measurements, hydraulic support pressures, dust suppression gauges, roadway centre lines, conveyor alignments, tensioning devices, safety appliances and looking for potential delays became very boring. But these observations were vital. It was a period in my working life that was so good, I never wanted it to end and so I would do everything possible to make sure it didn't.

It eventually did end, however, with the arrival of a new general manager. He decided that, due to the improvements made to the locomotive man riding transport, which enabled men to arrive at the coalface several minutes early, the bonus incentive norm for the team of workmen should be raised. He also decided that it was time a second team of men were put on to the face.

Putting a second team of men on to the face was common sense, but to increase the incentive norm, meaning more cuts had to be taken before the men got their bonus, was real stupidity. In the long term there was no way that the men would accept the increase.

Over the years, I had been in the privileged position of using my experience to give advice to senior management. But, alas, not any more. I now considered the senior management at the colliery to be arrogant, stupid, and downright discourteous.

After the bonus norm changed, the men only made a substantial bonus during three weeks of the following 12 months. We were now back in the position where one shift blamed the other. Deliberate guerrilla tactics were being employed, machinery was being deliberately sabotaged, production delays were high, and relations between the men and the officials turned sour. On numerous occasions, production from two shifts of men was less than it had been when only one team of men worked the face. The incentive bonus peak of £25 a shift dropped dramatically, and the couldn't-care-less attitude prevailed once again. Indiscipline was rampant.

It was obvious to me that the high bonus earnings of the past were now being used to pay the wages of the second team of men. Conditions on the face deteriorated, powered supports became buried and had to be dug out, the face conveyor became undulated and was graded using wooden props, the coal thickness indicator rarely worked, and cutting the floor and the roof was once again determined by guess work.

By nature I am a worrier, and to see men deliberately not trying left me feeling depressed. Here we had a situation where one of the most sophisticated modern coalfaces in the world, was being deliberately abused by both the men and senior management and, like it or not, as an official I was piggy in the middle. Informing senior management of the men's attitudes, using their exact words, such as 'We've thrown in the towel' and 'You're getting nowt', I was just told not to worry and to let them stew in their own mire. 'Bloody hell,' I thought, 'Here we have a face that cost around two million pounds and senior management are not concerned'.

At about the same time as this, the face on the south side of the district, under the retreat system, was also in dispute and the men were deliberately not trying because they said that the incentive norm was too high. I was told that the area director was coming to see for himself why production was so low. After his visit he apparently told the under-manager that he should be asking the manager to lower the incentive norm to a more realistic level. I really thought that because of this incident, the manager should have been sacked. However, in the mining hierarchy of the NCB, management were never sacked; they were either moved sideways or promoted to another area.

It seemed to me that for the area director to come to the colliery and make that kind of comment was a poor reflection on his own judgement, after all, he was responsible for appointing the man in the first place.

I won't tell you what I thought of the way he managed things!

The previous general manager had managed the colliery very efficiently: by that I mean that the colliery was bursting at the seams with coal (excuse the pun), workmen were receiving bonuses averaging £55 a week plus their basic wage, and everyone was happy.

I was officially appointed colliery overman on 4 July 1983, several months after my initial appointment. It was a strange experience. I was summoned to the deputy manager's office on his last day at Westoe; he had been appointed general manager at a colliery in Durham. He was a smashing bloke who talked my language. He thanked me for my help and co-operation and then offered me the colliery overman's job. We shook hands and I left his office.

The following Monday I was again summoned to the deputy manager's office and informed by the acting deputy manager that my appointment had been cancelled for the time being. I was thunderstruck. I told him of my conversation with the previous deputy manager regarding my appointment, but all he said was that he was in charge now and he would be making the necessary appointments.

I had no regard for the acting deputy manager, but he assured me that I would be appointed overman in the near future. However, this did not materialise. Although I was carrying out the duties of a colliery overman, I was not officially appointed and I had an uneasy feeling that I was not part of the Westoe 'mafia'. Eventually I went to the new deputy manager and asked him why I had not been given the job; within days my appointment came through.

The colliery overman's job is to take charge of the under-manager's district in his absence. Most collieries work with a colliery overman covering each shift, but at Westoe they only covered two of the four shifts which, to me, was not in the best interests of the pit.

By becoming colliery overman I had now reached the pinnacle of a miner's career. To go any further up the promotion ladder I would need qualifications as an under-manager or a Class II certificate.

It always seemed strange to me that a colliery overman was capable of being in charge during holiday periods, when it suited senior management, but without official qualifications he could never be permanently appointed as an under-manager. With some managers, this made me feel like a second class citizen.

Shift superintendents, or shift under-managers as they were commonly called, were slowly taking over the colliery overman's job.

These were lads with first or second class mining certificates who were waiting to become under-managers. And in this role they were gaining valuable experience by taking notice of the colliery overman's skills and expertise in man-management.

I could usually tell whether or not these lads would make it, simply by watching their behaviour. Some were highly intelligent but lacked confidence due to inexperience. Some had sufficient experience but had been misguided during an era of bad techniques and constant pressure from senior management (usually the deputy manager) to produce coal at all costs, and lacked the character to stand up for their own principles. Deputy managers were usually of such a strong character that very few officials under them challenged their words of command.

Having achieved the position of colliery overman, I spent every Saturday morning (during the 6am to 12 noon shift) at the surface going over the bonus and pay sheets making sure that the workmen, mechanics and officials were given the correct rate of pay and the proper bonus. I worked with the office staff, and once I'd signed the sheets they were then counter-signed by the under-manager.

Quite often during this shift I would be summoned to the deputy manager's office, usually to receive a bollocking for something or other. But on one occasion he asked me in to discuss what I thought of his new face design for the next production unit. He told me that he was thinking of installing a Dosco road machine to drive the face tail-gate in front of the face.

I just couldn't believe it. He was planning to install a machine costing over £500,000 to cut the tail-gate roadway in advance of the face, when I had proved on the last production face that the face machine was capable of doing this exact job. His decision was completely nonsensical. Anyway for some reason he must have had second thoughts and abandoned the idea.

8 The strike of 1984-5

On September 1 1983 Ian McGregor was appointed chairman of the NCB. I felt that with his knowledge and experience of running coal mining companies in America he was just the man needed to sort out senior management and the unions.

It was obvious to me, and other officials at Westoe, that it would not take long for a confrontation to develop between the chairman and the NUM. Coals were being stockpiled on the surface in the pit yard, underground pumps were being changed to remote control, and we were waiting for the big bang to happen, that is, for the unions to start fighting.

The big bang came on March 1, 1984 with the closure of Corton Wood Colliery in Yorkshire. At the same time McGregor revealed his plans to cut back production by 4,000,000 tons a year and to cut the work force by dispensing with 20,000 workmen. It was just the platform 'King Arthur' Scargill had been waiting for. 'Get off your knees!' was his cry to the miners. 'Fight for your job, and the jobs of your children and grandchildren'. What a first class idiot!

There must be something wrong with a society that was still sending men down to work in these conditions when it could be avoided. It was obvious to me that Arthur was being 'set up', yet it appeared he couldn't see it.

'Here we go again,' I thought. More pit closures like the ones in the sixties, except this time large posters offering redundancies of £1,000 for every year of service at the coalface to all men up to the age of 50 were being displayed around the colliery just days before the strike began. Had it been a Labour government offering these redundancy payments, things might have turned out very differently.

However, as history has proved, McGregor had given Scargill the red flag he wanted to start a bullfight! Years earlier, when I first noticed Arthur Scargill, I thought that he was just the man the industry needed to shake up senior management. But my thoughts soon changed when I discovered that his ranting and raving was not in keeping up with changing times. We were both born in 1938 and started work in 1953. My university of life was the coalface, his the union.

I often think that, had Arthur been born 40 years earlier, he probably would have been well placed to do an awful lot of good for the miners of the day. However, in the 1980s, his aspirations were well out of date. I suspect that, had he been born in the Victorian era, he would have fought long and hard for children to keep their jobs as chimney sweeps while placing an electric brush in their hands to ease their job.

In my own experience, when a colliery is closed the community does not die with it. Having witnessed dozens of collieries close around my own home, I did not see communities go under. People make up a community, not a colliery. When a pit closes the heart misses a beat, but life does go on.

It was during the strike, and while writing this book, that I was approached in my local pub by an old ex-miner. He told me that as a young miner during the 1926 strike he was a black-leg; he either had to do that or starve. While we were chatting he suddenly began to recite a poem of that era. After listening to him I asked him where he'd learnt it and he said his mother used to recite it when he was a boy. 'Could you write it down for me?' I asked, 'I can't be bothered with that,' he said, 'but I'll recite it for you and you can write it down.' I got the impression that he couldn't write but I didn't like to ask him.

I don't know who the poet was but I was fascinated by it. It goes like this:

Out of sight of God's bright sunshine,
Out of reach of God's pure air,

Down below in the realms of darkness,
There the miner does his share.
Not for him the bird sings sweetly,
Nor the flowers blooming fair,
But in half illumed darkness,
There the miner does his share.
Ever facing unseen danger,
Death the reaper does not spare,
Heeding but the call of duty,
There the miner does his share.
Now he's threatened with reduction,
In a wage already bare,
Miner, wife and little children,
Each would have their lesser share.
O ye working men of Britain,
Do you realise or care,
Please help to keep them from starvation,
Hunger is so hard to bear.

Obviously, Mr McGregor soon realised that the senior management of the NCB had surrendered to the unions and one of the main problems facing the industry was bad management. Westoe colliery was typical of the country as a whole, there were too many faces, too many machines, and too many men. Westoe had six production faces employing, at its peak, 2,400 men producing just over 1 million tons of coal and yet it just managed to break even. From my own experience, I knew that given the right management and the right workforce, with the right attitudes, the same production of 1 million tons a year could be achieved with half the workforce. After all, at the Havannah we were producing 500,000 tons of coal with 1,000 men in three-and-a-half feet seams, whereas at Westoe some seams were as high as seven-and-a-half feet, making conditions much easier.

I used to think that Westoe had become simply a place of employment with coal mining as a sideline. Some of the workforce were ex-miners who had returned to Westoe simply because they could not find employment elsewhere. How on earth did they get past the personnel department? It seemed to me that anyone with two arms and two legs was being employed. Small wonder that we were achieving 1960s results with 1980s machinery and technology!

To employ 2,400 men and manage to break even at the end of the financial year was quite an achievement. But I knew we could achieve the same tonnage with half the workforce. This would mean that 1,400 men would be placed on the dole, but at the same time the colliery would then be making profits in excess of £10 million. In my opinion, management were subject to their political masters. A Labour government would have gone for full employment and no profit, the Tories would go for high profits by squeezing the workforce.

Ian McGregor would look at this purely from the businessman's point of view. I knew that in the end competition from other countries would dictate policy over here. If the coal industry had any chance of surviving it would have to start making profits. American mines using British technology were achieving mind-boggling results. It was about time we did likewise.

As far back as 1970 I attended a lecture at Ashington Technical College on aspects of American mining. It was given by Coal Board officials who had visited several coalfields in America. What I heard was unbelievable.

They told me that the largest coal company in America was the Capstan Coal Company which operated strip mining (we call it open-cast) on a scale almost impossible to imagine in this country. The coalfield was situated in Pennsylvania and the area they had to work was equivalent to the size of Wales.

There was one crane on site, built to their own specifications, that cost $13 million. It could lift 1,000 tons of coal in one swoop. 500 men were employed and they produced seven million tons of coal a year.

To illustrate the size of this monster we were shown a slide of an average American saloon car at the base of one of the crane wheels. It looked like a Dinky toy in comparison. The nearest we had in this country was in South Northumberland on the Butterwell site, near Morpeth. It cost £2 million and could lift 200 tons of coal in one swoop. It was said to be the biggest of its kind in Europe.

For underground mining in this country to compare with American strip mining was just not on. No wonder they could mine it, and then ship it anywhere in the world and still only charge half of our pithead price.

March 6, 1984 was the beginning of the notorious miners' strike. Due to the very militant workforce at Westoe, senior management were so experienced in dealing with disputes and potential strikes that their plan of action had been prepared in advance. They agreed to a deal with my union, NACODS, who were not on strike, whereby a token number of officials would approach the picket line at the start of every shift as though they were going to work. But every time, having talked to the pickets, they would refuse to cross the picket line and then return home. This was to be the pattern for the next 12 months.

As we, as a union, were not in dispute with the coal board, they were duty bound to pay us. So, twice a week I had to make a round trip of 60 miles to present myself for work, knowing full well that I would not be crossing the picket line, to earn my week's wages. However, during the strike my income was halved because I was not doing any overtime or receiving any expenses. But it was a damn sight more than I got at the Havannah during the 1974 strike.

Just about every other week we attended union meetings to receive updates on local and national developments from our union representatives. On April 11, NACODS voted in favour of a strike over pit closures by 55 per cent, but because it was not passed with the required two-thirds majority, we remained officially in work.

Our practice of turning up at the picket line at the beginning of every shift enabled senior management to enjoy a trouble free existence with virtually no hassle for most of the strike. Had any NACODS members crossed the picket line all hell would have been let loose. No doubt senior management were quite pleased with the way things were progressing – very little trouble on the picket lines and all major and minor underground pumps and fans being monitored by remote control. In fact, the picket lines had become so quiet that at one of our frequent NACODS meetings one of our members complained that the last time he turned up for work there was only one man and a pram on the picket line! So our union secretary had a word with the NUM secretary and more pickets were organised.

As all was quiet on the Westoe front; this enabled the Westoe lads, who were probably among the most militant in the country, to roam around other coalfields in buses and cars and help create the scenes of violence that were shown daily on the evening news. Sadly they were fighting for a lost cause, a cause they could never win.

Pit closures, which were the main grievance of the strikers, were first undertaken by a Labour government during the 1960s, but in those days the NUM didn't have anyone who could whip up such ferocity amongst the workers as Arthur Scargill could in the 1980s. Arthur Scargill's talk of 'hit lists' was nothing new. On both my deputy's course and the overman's course, lecturers told us of projected closures for the North East. However, the media didn't give these lists quite the attention Arthur Scargill got!

I felt very sorry for the lads who were being easily led by Scargill; the silent majority was stifled because they had no one to champion them. The voice of moderation had deserted them. Ten per cent of NUM workers eventually became officials and were absorbed into NACODS. Anyone with a degree of common sense, especially if they had been involved with the strikes in 1972 and 1974, joined the Deputies' and Officials' union, leaving the militants to rampage through the NUM.

A typical example of what I mean is provided by a man for whom I had tremendous admiration, a fellow colliery overman at Westoe. Billy was a strapping six footer who could be as hard as nails or as gentle as a lamb and was respected by the majority of men at the colliery. He was a complete miner who relished a challenge and thrived under pressure. He was the epitome of common sense and his only fault, in my opinion, was that he tended to err on the side of the workmen.

I'm told that during the 1972 and 1974 strikes he gained admiration from all of the workforce at Westoe; he was their natural leader and spokesman.

He had so much respect for, and loyalty to, the NUM that it took him months of agonising before he could make the decision to leave the NUM and join NACODS in order for him to become an official. Once he had made the decision to leave, it opened the floodgates for other NUM followers to do the same.

He was a natural orator with a gift of the gab. I always felt that his immense talent was being wasted and should have been put to good use elsewhere. During debates he could get up in front of 200 men and win them over simply with facts, reason and common sense. On several occasions I found myself deciding which way I was going to vote on a certain issue only to be swayed by Billy's oratorical powers and persuasion.

I am sure that his blind loyalty to the NUM delayed his progress to promotion, he could have become an official much earlier and gone on to a much higher level if only he had left the NUM sooner. Like myself, he was one of a rare breed of miners who had fallen in love with mining. His passion for the job was obvious; he was a true mining professional whose university of life was the coalface. As a member of the NUM he was often asked to stand as Union Secretary or Chairman but always had to say 'no' in case the post might interfere with his passion for the blood, sweat and fear of the coalface. This may sound very strange to people who are not associated with coal mining but it is something I totally understand, it is a feeling that comes from deep within your heart like a religion.

From April to August the fortnightly meetings of the NACODS union were much concerned with run-of-the-mill stuff. In August, the NCB distributed a circular informing deputies that they were to cross over the picket lines or lose their pay. The NACODS executive immediately called a strike ballot. A member of the Durham area executive of NACODS addressed us at a union meeting outlining the case for strike action. He saw fit to tell us what a big bad bully Ian McGregor was, and also to point out that some of our members were afraid to cross the picket line for fear of intimidation, a situation that was not acceptable in this day and age.

Our union had never been militant before, but now the time was ripe for us to take action. If we really used our muscle we could call our members throughout the country, including those still working in Nottingham and Lancashire. As the dispute later proved, we held the real power in mining.

I asked the executive delegate, 'If we give you the power to strike, how will you use that power?' He replied that the strike would be over within two weeks and he was willing to bet anyone in the hall £5 on that. 'I'll take your bet,' I shouted from the back of the hall, only to be rebuked by the chairman for talking whilst the executive delegate was on his feet.

The ballot resulted in a massive 83 per cent in favour of a strike, resulting in a climb down by the Coal Board who said the circular issued had been based on a misunderstanding. The Coal Board capitulated to all NACODS demands. They later issued a statement saying that the Coal Board's proposals, which were announced on March 6 for the closure of pits and reduction in manpower, would have to be reconsidered because of the loss of production that had occurred as a result of the dispute. A new independent review body would be set up to consider all pit closures and its view would be given full weight.

Well, in my opinion our national delegates had really messed it up. Although they had achieved all our demands as a union, their main purpose had been to end the strike and at that moment, with the government at our mercy, instead of recommending an end to the strike they made the mistake of using it as a weapon to bargain with. This prolonged the dispute by a further four months and it finally ended on March 5, 1985, almost a year to the day after it started.

Just before Christmas 1984 a small trickle of men started to return to work. They had to be bussed in with police escorts and the pickets were so violent that the buses had to be reinforced with wire mesh on the windows to protect the men from flying bricks that were being hurled in their direction. Because of this violence, NACODS members refused to cross the picket line even in armoured buses. We were not going to argue with pickets who had been provided with barrels of ale to give them false courage!

Eventually, with more and more men returning to work, it was time to stand up and be counted. A skeleton crew of officials would report for work at the beginning of each shift, and they would walk through the picket line instead of being bussed through. I was a member of the crew that went through on the very first occasion. We lined up like soldiers with two policemen to escort us through, one at the front and one at the rear. I don't remember there being many pickets present but it seemed that there were thousands, 'Scabs! scabs! scabs!' they shouted, punching the air with their fists at the same time. The noise was deafening and the atmosphere was electric.

I've been through picket lines before but none of them compared to this. Although no one was accosted, having men, women and children screaming at me was a very strange sensation. At the time I didn't feel fear, only a very strange sense of excitement. I don't know how I looked but some of the lads were deathly white and two of them actually re-crossed the picket line and returned home petrified.

Once inside the main building, a voice inside me kept repeating

'Sanctuary, sanctuary', then I realised that although we were in, we had no idea how we were we going to get out. Once underground I instructed all of my officials to examine every part of the mine under our jurisdiction. I wanted to examine the two production faces myself. The only workforce I had at my command were a few men to repair or renew conveyor joints on the trunk roads.

After examining both faces I was amazed to find that the conditions were exactly the same as they would have been had we been away for only the weekend. The roadways were in a similar condition. It was unbelievable. Weeks before, the general manager had been on television stating that the pit was dying. Well, he must not have visited my district because it was no different from the way it had been 12 months before, although to be fair to him there had been water problems at the shaft.

After returning to the surface and having a bath we once again marched through the picket lines, and this time we experienced a lot less hostility. We had our cars parked in side streets away from the pit and quickly made for home. I knew then that it was just a matter of days before it would be all over. Westoe, perhaps one of the most militant collieries, stayed out until the bitter end. The miners eventually marched back to work in a triumphant fashion waving their flag.

Relations between the workers and officials at Westoe were never very friendly, even before the strike. I think this was due to the fact that the officials received an upstanding wage and statutory overtime. I was not looking forward to returning to work with the men. However, the atmosphere was not as hostile as I thought it would have been. I could sense that the men were relieved to be back at work, even though some of them were loath to take orders at first. However, they knew there was nothing they could do about it.

Once back to work, the men were given no indication from their union on how to react with fellow workers. After the last strike in the Gormley era they were told to settle their differences over a pint, but this was a different kettle of fish altogether. On this occasion some of the workers who had returned to work during the strike were victimised for being scabs. I have never witnessed a more intense hatred between people than that between these two factions of mine workers. What made it even more difficult was that some of these men had to work side by side, and it was part of my job to see that they did so. But how on earth could I supervise men that didn't even speak to each other?

In the next few weeks I was to witness things that I never thought one man could do to another. One man put his hand in his jacket pocket to take out his bait only to find that it had been replaced by human excrement. Another man had his clothes ripped to shreds with a Stanley knife. Water bottles were urinated in and obscene messages scrawled on toilet walls. The comradely spirit that had previously existed just disappeared. Workers separated themselves into two groups, us and them. They tried to travel in separate man-riding cars to and from their places of work, and on occasions men deliberately missed the cage rather than have to travel with a scab. If men from each group had to work together, invariably the job was never finished. Each man blamed the other for not doing what he should, all to the detriment of production. I could see it was going to be a long time before relations between the two groups ever got back to normal, if they ever did. One young lad, an electrician, told me that he was being branded as a scab by his mates after being off work for 50 weeks during the strike because he came back to work one week early.

The next couple of weeks were spent getting the men re-accustomed to their working environment, in other words letting them get their pit legs back. After all, 12 months is a long time. A plan was drawn up by senior management for the testing of all electric motors and cables. This involved a tremendous amount of physical labour, but I suppose it helped the men and officials get back into the swing of things.

An enormous number of rollers and conveyor joints had to be replaced; the cost must have been enormous. Literally hundreds of boxes of couplings were used, so many, in fact, that the stores both underground and at the surface both ran out, probably the first time in mining history.

Approximately five weeks after the strike the men's attitude to work was still low and production delays were frequent. Very little coal was being produced and something had to be done to bring the problem to a head. I went on to one production face to find that the machine operators were deliberately shearing at a rate of three feet a minute, instead of the normal 16 feet a minute. After a few enquiries it was plain to me that the men were not bothered whether any coal was produced or not. Apathy was everywhere. What made the situation worse, as far as I was concerned, was the fact that conditions were almost perfect.

I was so incensed that I locked off the face conveyor and switched off the power to the machines. I contacted my district under-manager and told him what I had decided to do; on his instruction I informed the district deputy and overman to dock the men's pay. I then left the district with the face standing idle and returned to the surface. I didn't feel proud of what I had done, but I knew in my heart that someone had to make a stand sooner or later.

Well, it certainly worked. The men had their pay suspended for a couple of weeks but were eventually reimbursed when things improved. All, that is, except for one man, the machine operator, who lost part of a shift's pay. However, he had the last laugh as his mates had a whip-round for him and he received more than his usual pay. But that didn't bother me as production steadily got back to normal and my 'kick up the backside' action was just what was needed. After that the men held no grudge.

In my mining career I have had many disputes with men but I could never understand the actions of senior management. Although I had been the cause of mini strikes and walkouts, while trying to establish my right to manage, I was never called upon in the negotiations to resolve the disputes. It was like being represented in court by a solicitor only I was not present. I felt that senior management thought that officials didn't know how to conduct themselves properly.

Over the years we had found many proven methods of production, but despite this we were now getting machinery and technology pushed into the mines at an alarming rate. Every new face was of a new design and was installed with bigger and better equipment. It seemed as if money couldn't be poured down the shaft fast enough. I felt it was like running a taxi business; you didn't have to buy Rolls Royces in order to run it efficiently. Having proved that machinery could do the job, more and more expensive equipment was being introduced. It was now costing over £3 million to install and equip a new production unit.

To my disgust, the expensive new equipment was never fully utilised. For example, on one face we had a set of prototype supports that cost in the region of £2 million and were intended to last for ten years, however, after four years they were written off and left on the face. I asked the deputy manager how on earth could such a flagrant misuse of tax-payers' money be allowed to take place and he told me that it wasn't our problem. 'What about salvaging them?' I suggested. 'We've got plenty on our plates at the moment so forget about it.' I asked the district's mechanical engineer what state the powered supports were in and he said that they were perfect. 160 powered roof supports costing £12,000 each were written off. Like me, the engineer thought the waste was criminal, especially as a manager worked to a five year colliery plan and ten year outline plan. (Or so I was led to believe.)

At the same time as the powered roof supports were written off, we were installing a new type of remotely operated system that meant if there was any delay on the outbye-conveyor, coal was diverted into a new roadway and stored there until it could be loaded. I just couldn't understand the logic behind this plan! Coal was being won out when it wasn't required and then transported to a purpose-built storage road. Why didn't they just leave the coal in its natural state at the face, and mine it when it was needed instead of going to all this unnecessary expense?

The men's attitude had changed for the better and face delays were almost eliminated. The main delays were now due to the fact that the pit was overproducing and individual faces were prevented from reaching their potential, too many faces and too many roadway machines were in production. It was just plain crazy.

The strike had established the colliery manager's right to manage, yet in my opinion we were still overmanned. As I have said before, the same production could be achieved using only half the workforce. The manager at Westoe seemed at a loss as to what to do but redundancies had to be made. However, at a senior staff meeting all heads of department were summoned to the area director's office. When the director referred to the future of Westoe, I was told that he banged his fist on the table to emphasise the point that Westoe would continue to employ 2,000 men. Perhaps he was waiting for a change of government that did not materialise. But at least I knew now why colliery managers had been economical with the truth in the past.

As colliery overman I was now in charge of the under-manager's district in the 5/4 seam. I was responsible for the production in the advancing face while Billy D. was responsible for the retreat face. Production from the two faces was in excess of 4,000 tons a day and each face worked only ten hours a day, in different shifts. The retreat face could have produced all the output if required working four shifts, (20 hours), without the other face.

Imagine two identical supermarkets each side of a High Street, one open when the other closed, both operating two shifts daily five days a week. We were getting very near the time when one coalface, with the right planning, design and under the retreat system, could produce the whole of the colliery's output. But in no way was this going to happen under the current management. If we were going to be competitive we had to reduce the workforce and the capacity. As far as I could see there was no other way to survive.

Thirty years ago Lord Robens had introduced the theory of

continuous mining. Technology had caught up with this theory, but the management still failed to address it.

Quite often visitors came underground at Westoe, sometimes it would be high ranking government officials and sometimes they would be the top brass from the Coal Board. On most occasions at least a week's notice of a visit was given by the under-manager. The higher the status of the visitor, the longer the time we had to prepare. For example, a production manager would command a week's notice whereas a deputy director would command at least a month. Much depended on exactly where the visit was due to take place.

Whenever I had to escort visitors underground it always reminded me of the time at Prestwick when I first had to escort two lads who wanted to see what conditions were like at the coalface as they were due to start work at the colliery the following week. My job was to take them underground, show them what conditions were like and then see them back to the shaft. To illuminate their path they had one candle between them. After walking about 20 minutes in a stooped position they had decided they'd had enough. 'I expected things to be hard, but this is only fit for idiots,' said one lad. They asked me to show them back to the shaft and that was the last anyone saw of them at Prestwick. It still makes me laugh now when I think about it.

Having discovered where the visit would take place, the under-manager would then scour the route and draw up a plan of action. In other words, we had a tidy-up campaign. The amount of men and materials required to prepare for one of these visits usually depended on how far the visitors would be travelling once underground. Preparations included remodelling the roads, stonedusting, painting, realigning conveyors, removing spillage and any other obstacles or scrap that might be lying in the roadway. The only thing we didn't do was to lay a red carpet. All of this was done to provide the visitor with the impression of a clean, efficient industry.

The cost of these tidy up campaigns could be astronomical, as sometimes even production was halted to ensure the manpower was available to carry out all the detailed jobs. If you added up the wages of the men plus the cost of lost production the total could run into tens of thousands of pounds. What other industry could afford to waste resources in this fashion? Mind you, having a major visit did wonders for the general tidiness of the district, a lick of paint and stone dust spread around a roadway not only brightened the place up but it made it a much nicer place in which to work.

I remember on one occasion, shortly after the 1984/85 strike, not only had tens of thousands of pounds been spent on a tidy-up campaign (as a high ranking member of the board was due to visit), but all senior officials of the district had to change their shifts to ensure the visit was a success. Each official was designated a roadway with a production conveyor in it, and it was his job to make sure the conveyor did not stop while the visit was taking place. He also had to make sure that no other workmen could be seen from the roadway.

It was such an important visit that the deputy manager of the colliery was instructed to go ahead of the visiting party in order to ensure that no workmen were visible from the visitors' route, and if necessary chase them from their place of work in order to ensure they could not be seen. This was to give the visitors the impression that the minimum of manpower was used underground. This impression was, of course, absolutely false. It was a prime example of not what was done but what had appeared to have been done, the colliery manager, once again, being economical with the truth. The wool was being completely pulled over the visitors' eyes.

I was told that the reason for the visit was to impress a top-ranking board member, so that he could give the go ahead for Westoe to spend more than £5 million on the next retreat production unit, with yet again a new face design. At my previous colliery, pit visitors did not command any attention at all.

On one occasion I was in the middle of a three-feet-high face trying to find out what was fouling the power loading machine. I was kneeling with my back wedged between the roof and the machine, when I felt something rather sharp poke me in the ribs. Turning round I found myself face-to-face or should I say nose-to-nose with a stranger. 'Who the bloody hell are you? And don't you do that again lad.' 'I'm the deputy director of mining,' he replied. 'I don't give a damn who you are, you're not poking me in the ribs.' 'I don't think much of your safety standards,' he said. 'What's the matter with them?' I asked. 'Self rescuers are meant to be worn at all times,' he said. 'I've got mine on,' showing him that it was strapped to my waist belt. 'One of the stonemen working on the tail-gate roadway has left his in his jacket pocket.' 'Oh! OK' I replied, and then he crawled past me. The general manager, who was grinning from ear to ear said, 'Howay John get this bloody machine away and get some coals on the belt for our visitors to see. Show him what we can do.' He then winked at me and crawled past, still grinning. Later on I heard that he was over the moon because I had stood up to the deputy director.

Shortly after the 1984/85 strike I decided that I'd had enough and I thought I'd try and get voluntary redundancy. I approached my union secretary and sounded him out, 'No chance' he said. At Westoe redundancy was going to be on a job-for-job basis and you couldn't be made redundant unless your job became redundant. However, a few weeks later he developed a heart condition and got his own redundancy.

I then approached the new deputy manager and asked him for redundancy. 'Why do you want it?' he asked. I explained to him that after 34 years in mining I'd had enough. The 64-mile round trip every day back and forwards to the colliery was starting to have its effect on me. Sometimes I was so tired after the early shift that I was falling asleep at the wheel of the car on the way home, and I had had several narrow escapes. They were becoming so frequent that on every journey home from work I would have to stop half way and freshen myself up. At the time I was working six or seven shifts a week and this was also having an effect on me. The deputy manager said he would see what he could do but wouldn't promise anything.

Eventually I made an appointment to see the general manager, but all he said was that he had a colliery to run and my job was part of the operational requirements of that colliery. I was rather annoyed because at that time my own district was running with an absenteeism rate of over 30 per cent and no one was doing anything about that.

At first I made no headway at all, and in the meantime a new redundancy agreement came out which offered the miners less than the first agreement. But I had made up my mind that I would take whatever was offered to me, even though this probably meant losing about £12,000, the difference between the two agreements. I let it be known throughout my district that I would take redundancy as soon as I could. Some of the officials and workmen told me that the Coal Board would never let me go. 'Why is that?' I asked. 'Because they can't do without you, you're too important a link in the chain.' 'Don't be daft,' I exclaimed. 'We're overmanned by 1,000 men and have four production units too many.' I suppose I should have been quite proud, but at that time all I wanted to do was to take my money and run. I think I was preparing myself for what I thought would be the eventual closure of Westoe if someone somewhere didn't take some action soon.

I kept on making appointments to see the general manager and I suppose I was making a bit of a nuisance of myself. I told him of a small business venture I had in mind and if my redundancy was not forthcoming I would lose out on the opportunity. He kept telling me that there was light at the end of the tunnel but he still had a pit to run. I also kept ringing the personnel manager, even though I knew it was a waste of time as he had no more say than I did, but at least it let everyone know that I was very keen to get out. Just to rub salt into my wounds over 2,000 staff at the area headquarters in Gateshead were being offered redundancy and apparently the Coal Board couldn't get enough volunteers; the area was so overmanned it was becoming an embarrassment. Just to give you some insight into what I mean, here is a list of just some of the people employed in the area:

Area Director
Deputy Director (Mining)
Deputy Director (Administration)
Chief Mining Engineer
Deputy Chief Mining Engineer
Area Industrial Relations Officer
Area Chief Engineer
Area Mechanical Engineer
Area Electrical Engineer
Area Civil Engineer
Regional Workshop Controller
Area Chief Draughtsman
Area Surveyor and Minerals Manager
Head of Provisioning/Technical Branch.
Area Mechanisation Engineer
Head of Safety and Environment
Area Purchasing and Stores Manager
Area Chief Scientist
Area Geologist
Area Method Study Engineer
Area Coal Preparation Engineer
Area Staff Manager/Secretary
Production Manager A District
Production Manager B District
Colliery Manager
Operations Engineer Mechanical A District
Operations Engineer Mechanical B District
Operations Engineer Electrician A District
Operations Engineer Electrician B District
Planner A District

Planner B District
Colliery Engineer Mechanical
Colliery Engineer Electrical
Colliery Surveyor
Colliery Safety Officer/Engineer
Colliery Ventilation Officer/Engineer
Colliery Dust Control Officer
Colliery Planner
Colliery Training Officer
Manager Training Centre
Mining Departmental Secretary
Solicitor (North East)
Area Medical Officer

After looking through this list my first thoughts were: 'My God, all these people have to be paid from the pick point as well!'

Technology was now moving at such a pace in the mine that it was difficult to keep track of what was happening. Yet I still couldn't fathom out why we didn't work our faces more intensively, apart from the fact that manpower would have to be greatly reduced. In fact there was an abundance of volunteers for redundancy. In my opinion, we could have worked four machine shifts on the one face instead of two machine shifts on both faces. As each face had to stand while the other one produced it was just plain crazy. I couldn't for the life of me understand the reasoning behind this other than the fact that the area director wanted to maintain a workforce of 2,000 men.

Over 4,000 tons per day was now being produced from my district. Such big outputs had to rely on the smooth running of machinery so monitoring was introduced, enabling repairs to be made at the pit's convenience. This system didn't eliminate breakdowns but maintenance at the face was of a much higher standard because it was being more closely monitored. For example, oil samples were taken from gearboxes and sent for analysis to measure the particles of steel present. The pit engineer could then plot the trend of machines and determine when a component part was likely to fail. Parts could be serviced before the breakdown occurred saving both time and money in lost production.

An environmental team had been formed to run electric cables from the surface control room, down the shaft, and seven miles out to the workings furthest away. The cost must have been phenomenal and I wanted to know why it was being done. Obviously it would make the environment ultra safe, but that meant they may as well do away with the deputy's job as most of his duties involved checking the environment.

Methane units were being installed to give off warning signals if too much methane was present in the air. Smoke detectors, which monitored levels of carbon monoxide and temperature and activated alarms that relayed back to the control room, were also being introduced. Auxiliary fans were being fitted with vibration analysers, which could cut off the power automatically if abnormal vibrations occurred. Development headings had instruments fitted to record air flows in the ventilation ducts. If the air flow reached a level below that set by the manager's ventilation rules it would activate an alarm. Air pressure units were installed and a fall in pressure caused warning lights to flash. Air velocity units were installed to record the quantity of air travelling across the coalface.

All this technology was good, great in fact, but at what cost? If used efficiently, this technology could mine coal with minimal intervention from human beings. In my opinion, there was sufficient manpower within the management engineer's mechanics sector to mine coal all by themselves. There were now far too many chiefs in the industry and not enough educated braves. The brains of the industry had to get off their backsides and get their hands dirty. The manager had to start to manage the colliery as a business; the days of playing at pits were over.

The future in mining, as I saw it was a series of small collieries with no more than two production units, all capable of high productivity, maximised by intensive continuous mining in one unit, with the second unit standing by to take over if production was delayed or after the main face had been exhausted. The key to this operation would be good management.

For all of my working life the miners had been promised bread and butter today and jam tomorrow. It took me a long time to realise that tomorrow never comes. For me the jam was to be my redundancy payment but I couldn't get it because I was too young (almost 50) with only 34 years experience!! At the time I was so confused and bitter, that after reading a circular from the area director I decided to write to him. My main topic was about the future of Westoe, because as I now saw it, as there was to be no change in the political master to rescue him from the situation, Westoe had no future if the management didn't start to take action now. The only way to save the colliery was to reduce the workforce.

Well, he thanked me for my letter and the interest I had shown and he said he was sending a copy to the manager of Westoe along with a letter from himself suggesting that I talk to him about wanting to leave the industry. This I did, and after three months of agonising and uncertainty I was finally made redundant in November 1987 (as was the general manager a few months later).

As I reflect on my life in the mines I find myself in the rare position of having experienced a wide range of coalface operations, having started work in conditions not far removed from the pit pony era and going right up to sophisticated cutting-edge technology of the 1980s including working seven miles from the shaft under the North Sea. I had been a part of changes that were so rapid that it was almost impossible to comprehend. The trouble was that we didn't have the people with the right attitudes to harness the technological changes effectively; both the unions and management saw to that.

Afterword

After I left the coal industry I started up on my own, first with a local milk business, then eventually purchasing two local newsagents, plus a third in Newcastle city centre. We also acquired the local Post Office and transferred it into the local paper shop. It became a very successful family business – not bad for a lad of humble beginnings.

The question often asked of underground coal miners is – would you send your sons down the mine? The answer is a definite NO, but, for myself, I would love to do it all again.

Our four grandchildren, Joseph, Rosie, Charlie and Grace will never fully understand my mining life, which in some ways I find quite sad. Mining passion is different from anything else. I can't explain it – I don't have the words. Maybe I have come some way towards it somewhere in my story.

The words I heard most often at the coalface were 'bloody idiot', provoked by anger, humour, or as an alternative to 'God bless you'. The dictionary defines 'idiot' as 'a born fool'. For generations miners survived inhuman conditions of work – wet, filthy, cramped, dangerous. Only fools would tolerate them, so the term 'bloody idiot' seems a more suitable description for the miner than the more heroic tributes that posterity might offer. I should know – I was a first class one!

John Graham, 2009

A short glossary of some terms used in this book

AFC - armoured face conveyor or flexible conveyor

bait - packed provisions

bank - the surface

banksman - surface worker at the cage

board and pillar system - where pillars of coal remain as supports

cage - lift to take men up and down shaft

caunch - space immediately above the coal face

caunchman - underground roadway maker

cavil - allocation of hewers' positions on the seam

chocks - powered roof supports

chummings - empty tubs

contraband - items forbidden underground for safety reasons

COSAS - Colliery Officials and Staff Association

creep - movement of the coal face

cross-gate - each tunnel running from the face joined into a single tunnel (the cross-gate)

CTI - coal thickness indicator

deputy - appointed by a manager to be in charge of an underground district

Dosco road header - tunneling machine

drift mine - a mine near the surface, accessed by sloping roadway

flat - where the haulage system ended

gate - roadway

goaf - the space in an abandoned tunnel which usually caves in

haulerman - works the winch in the engine house

heapstead - the top of the shaft

hew - cut coal at the face

highside - tunnels to right of main gate

inbye - towards the coalface

jib - cutting part of cutting machine

jigger - screening plant

jowelling - tapping the roof to detect fractures by sound

keps - iron bars to support underside of cage

kist - a chest for reports at the deputy's meeting station

longwall - coal face

lowside - tunnels to left of main gate

main-gate - the main roadway

marra - workmate

master shifter - colliery overman

NACODS - National Association of Colliery Overmen, Deputies and Shot-firers

NCB - National Coal Board

nog - temporary wooden support

NUM - National Union of Mineworkers

onsetter - puts full tubs into the cage to go to the surface

outbye - moving away from the face

overman- in charge of the day to day work at the colliery

putter - pushes empty tubs to and full tubs from the hewer

ripper - another name for stoneman

ripping lip

screening sheds

staple- vertical shaft between two seams

steel dregs - short steel bars

stoneman - maker and repairer of roadways

stonework - making and repairing roadways

tail-gate - return roadway for stale air from the face to the surface

tokens - metal strips attached to a tub to indicate its hewer

trepan shearer - cores out the centre of the coal seam for household coal

weighman - weighs tubs of coal at the surface

winding time - the time taken for the cage to travel up or down the shaft